# Palgrave Critical University Studies

Series Editor
John Smyth
University of Huddersfield
Huddersfield, UK

Universities everywhere are experiencing unprecedented changes and most of the changes being inflicted upon universities are being imposed by political and policy elites without any debate or discussion, and little understanding of what is being lost, jettisoned, damaged or destroyed. The over-arching intent of this series is to foster, encourage, and publish scholarship relating to academia that is troubled by the direction of these reforms occurring around the world. The series provides a much-needed forum for the intensive and extensive discussion of the consequences of ill-conceived and inappropriate university reforms and will do this with particular emphasis on those perspectives and groups whose views have hitherto been ignored, disparaged or silenced. The series explores the effects of these changes across a number of domains including: the nature of academic work, the process of knowledge production for social and public good, along with students' experiences of learning, leadership and institutional politics research. The defining hallmark of this series, and what makes it markedly different from any other series with a focus on universities and higher education, is its 'criticalist agenda'.

More information about this series at
http://www.springer.com/series/14707

Neil Cocks

Higher Education Discourse and Deconstruction

Challenging the Case for Transparency and Objecthood

Neil Cocks
Department of English
  and American Literature
University of Reading
Reading, UK

Palgrave Critical University Studies
ISBN 978-3-319-52982-0   ISBN 978-3-319-52983-7 (eBook)
DOI 10.1007/978-3-319-52983-7

Library of Congress Control Number: 2017932320

© The Editor(s) (if applicable) and The Author(s) 2017
This work is subject to copyright. All rights are solely and exclusively licensed by the Publisher, whether the whole or part of the material is concerned, specifically the rights of translation, reprinting, reuse of illustrations, recitation, broadcasting, reproduction on microfilms or in any other physical way, and transmission or information storage and retrieval, electronic adaptation, computer software, or by similar or dissimilar methodology now known or hereafter developed.
The use of general descriptive names, registered names, trademarks, service marks, etc. in this publication does not imply, even in the absence of a specific statement, that such names are exempt from the relevant protective laws and regulations and therefore free for general use.
The publisher, the authors and the editors are safe to assume that the advice and information in this book are believed to be true and accurate at the date of publication. Neither the publisher nor the authors or the editors give a warranty, express or implied, with respect to the material contained herein or for any errors or omissions that may have been made. The publisher remains neutral with regard to jurisdictional claims in published maps and institutional affiliations.

Cover pattern © Melisa Hasan

Printed on acid-free paper

This Palgrave Macmillan imprint is published by Springer Nature
The registered company is Springer International Publishing AG
The registered company address is: Gewerbestrasse 11, 6330 Cham, Switzerland

Series Editor's Preface

Naming this as a Critical University Studies Series gives it a very distinct and clear agenda. The over-arching intent is to foster, encourage, and publish scholarship relating to universities that is troubled by the direction of reforms occurring around the world.

It is a no-brainer that universities everywhere are experiencing unprecedented changes. What is much less clear, and there are reasons for the lack of transparency, are the effects of these changes within and across a number of domains, including:

- The nature of academic work
- Students' experiences of learning
- Leadership and institutional politics
- Research and the process of knowledge production, and the
- Social and public good

Most of the changes being inflicted upon universities globally are being imposed by political and policy elites without any debate or discussion, and little understanding of what is being lost, jettisoned, damaged or destroyed. Benefits, where they are articulated at all, are framed exclusively in terms of short-term political gains. This is not a recipe for a robust and vibrant university system.

What this series seeks to do is provide a much-needed forum for the intensive and extensive discussion of the consequences of ill-conceived and inappropriate university reforms. It does this with particular emphasis on those perspectives and groups whose views have hitherto been ignored, disparaged or silenced.

The defining hallmark of the series, and what makes it markedly different from any other series with a focus on universities and higher education, is its 'criticalist agenda'. By that we mean, the books raise questions like:

- Whose interests are being served?
- How is power being exercised and upon whom?
- What means are being promulgated to ensure subjugation?
- What might a more transformational approach look like?
- What are the impediments to this happening?
- What then, needs be done about it?

The series intends to foster the following kind of contributions:

- Critical studies of university contexts, although they might be local in nature, are shown to be global in their reach;
- Insightful and authoritative accounts that are courageous and that 'speak back' to dominant reforms being inflicted on universities;
- Critical accounts of research relating to universities that use innovative methodologies;
- Looking at what is happening to universities across disciplinary fields, and internationally;
- Examining trends, patterns and themes, and presenting them in a way that re-theorizes and re-invigorates knowledge around the status and purposes of universities; and
- Above all, advancing the publication of accounts that re-position the study of universities in a way that makes clear as to what alternative robust policy directions for universities might look like.

The series aims to encourage discussion of issues like academic work, academic freedom, and marketization in universities. One of the shortcomings of many extant texts in the field of university studies is that they attempt too much, and as a consequence their focus becomes diluted. There is an urgent need for studies in a number of aspects with quite a sharp focus, for example:

1. There is a conspicuous absence of studies that give existential accounts of what life is like for students in the contemporary university. We need to know more about the nature of the stresses and

strains, and the consequences these market-driven distortions have for the learning experiences of students, their lives and futures.
2. We know very little about the nature and form of how institutional politics are engineered and played out, by whom, in what ways, and with what consequences in the neoliberal university. We need 'insider' studies that unmask the forces that sustain and maintain and enable current reform trajectories in universities.
3. The actions of policy elites transnationally are crucial to what is happening in universities worldwide. But we have yet to become privy to the thinking that is going on, and how it is legitimated and transmitted, and the means by which it is made opaque. We need studies that puncture this veil of silence.
4. None of what is happening that is converting universities into annexes of the economy would be possible without a particular version of leadership having been allowed to become dominant. We need to know how this is occurring, what forms of resistance there have been to it, how it has been suppressed, and the forms of solidarity necessary to unsettle and supplant this dominant paradigm.
5. Finally, and taking the lead from critical geographers, there is a pressing need for studies with a focus on universities as unique spaces and places—possibly in concert with sociologists and anthropologists.

We look forward to this series advancing these important agendas and to the reclamation and restitution of universities as crucial intellectual democratic institutions.

John Smyth
Professor of Education and Social Justice
University of Huddersfield &
Emeritus Professor, Federation University Australia

Acknowledgments

Contemporary university structures increasingly favour those willing and able to position themselves as 'academic entrepreneurs'. Fortunately, there are those in the sector who are not taken in by such Tory narratives. Here I am thinking especially of Dr. Jessica Medhurst, whose generosity, integrity and commitment to cutting-edge academic critique continues to inspire so many.

As always, this book is rooted in conversations with colleagues and friends at CIRCL, the Graduate Centre for International Research in Children's Literature: Literature, Culture, Media at The University of Reading. Thanks especially to Karin Lesnik-Oberstein, Sue Walsh, Ian Mulholland, Krissie West, and Haleemah Ziarab. Thank you also to Prof. David Brauner.

Thanks to Wig for her commitment to teaching and artistic practice in the face of reductive managerialsm. And lots of love as well. . . .

I am indebted to Dr. Daniel Watt and James Scott for helping me develop my thinking on education. And thank you once again to John McGrath, who set me on the path.

CONTENTS

1 Introduction: Transparency and Objecthood   1

2 '[...] Not much like a Grove [...]': Openness, Object, and *Agora* in 'The Lecherous Professor Revisited' by Diane Purkiss   17

3 Therapy and its Discontents: Bullying, Freedom and Self-Evidence in *The Dangerous Rise of Therapeutic Education* by Kathryn Ecclestone and Dennis Hayes   39

4 New-Managerial Ontology: Materiality, Vision and Disclosure in *Non-Representational Theory* by Nigel Thrift   63

Index   93

CHAPTER 1

Introduction: Transparency and Objecthood

Abstract The book begins with a widely disseminated anecdote concerning an email asking members of a university department to bring an object of which they are proud to a forthcoming meeting. It could be a publication or a sporting trophy. This will allow colleagues to witness the year's positive achievements, while also countering an increasingly reductive REF process. This introductory chapter reads the anecdote in a more critical fashion, and thus sets out the central thesis of the book: objects and openness are often taken to oppose managerial culture, yet they are also bound to its ongoing operation. Following the work of Bill Readings, it is claimed that the 'University of Excellence' requires a notion of unproblematic communication that notions of objecthood and transparency help to secure.

Keywords Higher education · Excellence · Objecthood

1   OBJECT AND AUDIT

I will begin with a story I have heard on numerous occasions at academic conferences across the United Kingdom over the past two years:

> Towards the end of a particularly difficult year, dominated by restructuring and the job losses that inevitably follow, lecturers within a university department receive an email from one of their managers. This suggests that

challenges at an institutional level threaten to divert attention from positive achievements. In order to celebrate success within the department, colleagues are asked to select an object of which they are particularly proud. These will be displayed together in a forthcoming departmental meeting. The object could be a new monograph, of course, but a sporting trophy or the fruit of some artistic endeavour would be of equal value. All objects should relate to recent activities, and need to be received by some central figure – an administrator, director of research or departmental head – at a given time prior to the meeting. If the significance of the object is unclear, a short explanatory note is to be attached.[1]

One can appreciate the reasoning behind such an exercise. Too often, it can seem, lecturers find themselves turning inward, unaware of their colleague's research and focused on an increasingly narrow idea of what constitutes work worthy of institutional recognition. The story could, however, be understood not so much as a celebration of community and diversity, but as indicative of many problems circulating within the contemporary UK university sector.

Take, for example, the idea that academic and non-academic objects are equally acceptable for display. Certainly, this might demonstrate an understanding of all that falls outside the 'bean-counting', dehumanising structures that dominate Higher Education. It can, however, also be figured as yet another move to erode the separation of public and private. All universities are keen to promote 'work-life balance', and an equality of value can certainly be read here, yet only in so far as the triumphs of home are subject to the auspices of the department.

A further issue, and one that is of more significance to this present book, is the insistence upon the 'object' common to all the versions of this narrative I have encountered. Again, although the range of objects that qualify for display can be understood to act as, say, a counter to the internal Research Excellence Framework (REF), where an ever smaller set of 'outcomes' are taken to be significant, it does not, I would suggest, escape a certain reductive, evidence-based frame. As personal pride must be attached to an object, it becomes open to display. One advantage of the object for this discourse is that it is constructed as sufficient, recognisable for what it is in a wholly unproblematic fashion. The monograph, as an object of pride, is displayed rather than read.[2] There is irony, then, in the insistence that certain other objects are in need of explanation. The collective display is about bringing pride and achievement into the open, where they can be seen, yet the visible sometimes requires a supplement. Indeed, it could be argued that even the monograph requires something other than itself: think, for example, of the email that frames the event or the audience's engagement with the objects displayed.[3]

As the objects are required to be deposited prior to the meeting, I would argue that a further discourse can be read, familiar to those working in the contemporary UK university. It is an instruction, after all, that limits the possibility of shock or subversion: absurd or inappropriate objects are unlikely to make it to the final event (Q: 'And what did you get this trophy for?' A: 'Two pound fifty at a car-boot'). The display of objects necessitates and calls upon an additional level of mediation, with openness managed through a repository. There is, in this, something of the strange logic of open access, at least in how it is realised within the university. I refer here to the recent HEFCE policy around REF submissions, requiring all work put forward for consideration in the assessment of academic outputs to be available to the public. The success of public engagement – and in an academic context, this is often a matter of whether a work has been read or not – is, in part, assessed through the fact of it having been archived. At my university, this process requires all relevant material to be placed in 'our institutional repository, CentAUR... a searchable electronic archive showcasing... recent research publications and outputs'.[4] In other words, it is only by a work being 'in' that it can be confirmed as 'out'. It is an operation that opens up a further level of institutional control, as not only is the depositing a task that must be completed, with success or failure addressed within Continuing Professional Development assessments, CentAUR is also where individual members of staff can find the results of internal REF reviews, although these grades are available only to them and a select number of academics charged with the overview of research outputs. The place of openness is, therefore, also a regulatory space, one partially closed. It would seem that bringing academic work to light necessitates a certain amount of darkness.

It is worth remarking here that if one were to decide to write an academic paper on one or more of the emails referenced earlier, it is likely that this ironic, partial illumination would once more be brought to ironic and partial light. Email is, after all, taken to be the property of the institution.[5] Although freedom of information requests can be used to access email accounts, with the institution increasingly empowered to take this action against its employees, any move to publish work concerning emails on computers and networks owned by the university will be contested.⁶ It follows that for many institutions, the public display of objects set up by the emails is one that is doubly obscured. It is a public display within the department only, and the email that acts as the frame should not come to public scrutiny. One consequence of this is that a detailed, academic reading of institutional correspondence is impossible. The researcher wishing to critique the terms used to enable and justify the departmental display must make do with generalisation. Without the specificity of the individual email, there can be no working through of the precise terms of its narration, the various perspectives and subject positions that it requires. Engagement must instead concern itself with a 'story' removed from the linguistic instance. I am concerned with the obscurity of the individual email not out of any wish to mourn lost objects, but because of the bar it places on *reading*. It is my claim that texts do not offer the certainty and stability of absence, but instead require reading as their necessary supplement. In what follows, I will suggest that such constitutive division is often resisted within a Higher Education discourse committed to the evidential. Take, for example, the previously discussed monographs constructed as objects of display, rather than texts to be read. Such objects can be understood by anyone. Pride and success are wholly available through a reckoning that moves effortlessly between the categories of leisured and professional achievement. As Bill Readings famously contends in *The University in Ruins*, this is the discourse of 'excellence' that structures the contemporary university, one that:

> responds very well to the needs of technological capitalism in the production and processing of information, in that it allows for the increasing integration of all activities into a generalized market, while permitting a large degree of flexibility and innovation at a local level. Excellence is thus the integrating principle that allows 'diversity' (the other watchword of the University prospectus) to be tolerated without threatening the unity of the system... Excellence draws only one boundary: the boundary that protects the unrestricted power of the bureaucracy. (Readings 1996, pp. 32–33)

I am suggesting that 'the object' does not offer an alternative to 'The University of Excellence' so conceived, although many early critics of new managerialism were committed to such an idea, and as we will read in Chapter 2, there are those that remain convinced of the possibility.⁷ Rather, the object is wonderfully suited to the culture of audit. It is, after all, taken to be supremely translatable, a presence that cannot be obscured or challenged by any discursive frame: interpret as you will, but concede to the independence of the thing. Conversely, as I have suggested, the object is also constructed as an absence within contemporary Higher Education discourse: in common with the institutional email, it promises a resistance to reading, remaining unseen, and thus beyond the power of detailed, specific critique.

I am, of course, not the first to challenge the culture of audit as it dominates university provision, at a global as well as national level. Stefen Collini, for example, argues that 'two of the most important sources of efficiency in intellectual activity are voluntary co-operation and intellectual autonomy. But these are precisely the kinds of things for which a bureaucratic system leaves little room' (Collini 2012, p. 134). Likewise, Richard House claims that ' "[a]udit culture" environments where the nature of learning is routinely specified and made explicit in advance are entirely antithetical to...an open learning milieu': the problem with a culture of clarity and evidence is that it cannot tolerate surprise, dynamism, or learning understood as a process of negotiation. Moreover, far from an addition to education, an invisible means of data collection, the hearing staged by audit impacts upon what is heard: 'the axioms of the audit-driven paradigm routinely influence, or even construct, the way in which practitioners and professionals conceive of, and think about, their work and their very identities within such regimes of truth' (House 2014).[8] As such, an audit is, as Bill Readings suggests through his reading of 'excellence', an institutional practice that flattens out difference.[9] For the smooth running of a central administration, what is heard in one location must be comparable to everything that might be encountered anywhere within its borders. Audit requires a single unit of currency that binds together diverse pedagogical practices, and it is this, it can be argued, that leads to an accounting culture, rather than a culture of accountability. The object of audit cannot be allowed to exceed its proper function. Moreover, as the Bologna Accords make clear, increasingly, comparison must extend even beyond institutional and national borders: freedom of movement and choice are taken to necessitate a centralised, extra-national structure.[10] One difficulty here is that the implementation of such universalising systems at a local level serves to perpetuate inequality, with Bologna accused of institutionalising Anglocentric understandings, and the introduction of:

> [n]ew hierarchies in university degrees, and thus the labour market...that contradict the goals of democratic education and employment policy...The knowledge...produced in the restructured universities is based on the

assumption that knowledge can be accelerated and optimised, that access to it can be controlled via patenting and monetisation and also that knowledge can only be coupled to concrete uses, for example the economic success of companies. The production and distribution of knowledge is to be re-ordered according to the principles of salesmanship.[11]

For Readings, the endless, self-affirming circulation of the closed terms of audit necessary to such 'reordering' and 'optimis[ation]' should be countered by a circulation whose endlessness is open. Rather than a quantifying system that privileges self-evidential display, Readings promotes the discursive, encouraging questions that are 'systematically incapable of producing cognitive certainty or definitive answers. Such questions will necessarily give rise to further debate, for they are radically at odds with the logic of quantification' (Readings 1996, p. 26). He also insists upon a radical otherness as necessary to teaching: the pedagogical scene can never be understood by a single participant within it, and again, this means that it can never be complete. It is the gap necessary to teaching – the aporia of the other – that structures its movement, a certain not-knowing that is necessary to thinking.

My goal in questioning audit culture is not that of returning the individual experience of the student, or even a specific cultural response, to an education narrowly focused on objective data. As I will be arguing in Chapter 3, in questioning the transparency of audit, I am not interested in promoting relativism, or in some other way reinstating the certainty of audience.[12] That would only be to install a finalizing presence at another stage of the pedagogical process. Rather, I aim, for example, to return the 'necessary supplement' of hearing to the discourse of audit, and thus to question the self-sufficiency of the object within Higher Education discourse.[13]

2   THE CHAPTERS

In what follows, my interest is with the seduction of audit; not with obviously reductive arguments, those emphasising the bottom-line to the exclusion of all else, but instead with those making a more vital or subtle case for installing objecthood and transparency at the centre of education provision. In one sense, this is nothing new: as far back as 1996, Bill Readings could claim that the university has a tradition of resisting arguments that too obviously import ideas from business. For example, academics are likely to question the undiluted language of Total Quality Management. For Readings, as indicated earlier, this is why terms like 'excellence' and 'diversity' are so important: as 'non-referential', they enable a closed, centralised system of management, yet in a way that few if any would think to criticise. I would suggest that in these times of austerity, bottom-line arguments are increasingly acceptable. Even so, no contemporary educational audit culture rests solely upon a claim to economic necessity. The three chapters that follow focus on texts that do not consistently criticise commercialism, yet understand Higher Education to be in need of reform, claiming that this can be achieved through a commitment to transparency and objecthood. It is variously claimed that such an approach can counter patriarchy within the institution, encourage innovation and experiment, and even oppose the worst excesses of managerialsim. The object is not understood to be part of the problem, but its solution. And that, I will be arguing, is its seduction.

I begin with a text that makes, I think, a particularly urgent case for the object, and also for an increasingly commercial education. 'The Lecherous Professor Revisited' by Diane Purkiss was published in 1994, and is a compelling critique of contemporary educational practice in universities, but especially the tutorial system at Oxford. Purkiss argues that a combination of one-to-one tutorials, a philosophical tradition that celebrates the reduplication of male authority, and a lack of discussion relating to teaching practice, make the sexual politics of the institution invisible, this forming a 'harraser's charter' (Purkiss 1994, p. 210). The tentative solution is to introduce a far more visible, public form of pedagogy. Taking her cue from the Athenian *agora*, Purkiss imagines an open space, a market of education, where students can come and go as they like, having no intense, sustained relationship with lecturers, who offer instead a series of digitally enhanced sessions, with 'seminars, tutorials and symposia [represented] as workshops, in which professors and students alike work to shape a variety of commodities, of which the student might be *one*' (Purkiss 1994, p. 210). Engaging a text written in the 1990s enables a reading of how such a vision came to be realised within the UK university sector. The idea of an educational marketplace featuring digitally enabled large-group teaching is one that has become all too prevalent, and has not, I would argue, overcome institutional sexism. To an extent, Purkiss recognises the dangers in pursuing a commercial education, but, as I have suggested, does not understand the object to be part of the problem. I read 'The Lecherous Professor Revisited' to be convinced by the promise of 'transparent' communication and community, as held out by 'The University of Excellence', sharing what Bill Readings takes to be the 'logic' of the 'majority of left-wing critics', that 'the egalitarian assumption at the heart of communicational transparency should be fully realized and that domination is an effect of failed communication' (Readings 1996, p. 183). In conclusion, I claim that 'The Lecherous Professor Revisited' attempts to achieve a purity of communication through the sacrifice of a 'scapegoat', the ejection of a derided element from the public space, as discussed by Jacques Derrida in his 'Plato's Pharmacy', a text upon which Purkiss's argument draws extensively. As Derrida suggests, the attempt to make the *polis* whole and clean is doomed: the rejected term always returns as constitutive of its other, even at the moment of perfection. There is, as Readings argues, an otherness in teaching that cannot be done away with, one that is not to be exhausted in the public, commercial, 'non-transcendent' objects upon which Purkiss pins her hopes for a liberated education.

Chapter 2 engages a text that rejects the political radicalism I read in Purkiss's work in favour of what Stephen Ball, for example, terms a 'restorationist agenda' (Ball 1994, p. 29). *The Dangerous Rise of Therapeutic Education* by Kathryn Ecclestone and Dennis Hayes challenges the increased focus upon feelings and their management within all areas of education provision in the United Kingdom. In turning from the external world, and focusing attention instead on the subjective experience of those entering the education scene, the suggestion is that contemporary pedagogy produces a 'diminished' learner.[14] For Ecclestone and Hayes, the trappings of new managerialism – whether learning contracts, self-reflexive Continuous Professional Development, or equality policies – are an expression of a relativistic rejection of objective reality: the truth is very much out there. It follows that despite arguing against the post-structuralism that informs much of the analysis forwarded by 'The Lecherous Professor Revisited', Ecclestone and Hayes can be understood to repeat that work's commitment to the logic of idealised community and communication.

To question this 'restorationist agenda', I find that I briefly have to widen my focus and read the account of 'bullying' in Higher, Further, and Primary Education offered by *The Dangerous Rise of Therapeutic Education*. For Ecclestone and Hayes, the widespread appeal to 'bullying' typifies what is wrong with contemporary pedagogy. It is understood to be an infantilizing term, one that encourages academics to think of injustice in 'playground' terms, rather than, for example, a matter of unionised dispute. It also encourages a self-centred outlook; a wallowing in emotion that is not helpful to anyone. In this I read a difficulty, as pulling oneself together in the pursuit of objective truth is fundamentally *healthy* for Ecclestone and Hayes. It is not that there is anything wrong with therapy in general, it would seem, the problem is that what gets classed as such falls short of its promise. There is a further difficulty, however, as I argue that an extended, detailed reading of 'bullying' within the text suggests that it is something other than a singular, real-world category, while also not simply an illusion. Rather, bullying, for Ecclestone and Hayes, is impossibly contradictory: it does and does not exist. Their claim is that the discursive has no place in university study. Education should focus on the facts. This is as advantageous as it is problematic for *The Dangerous Rise of Therapeutic Education*, I suggest, in so far as it is through a *reading* of the text that the defence of objecthood can be questioned.

I conclude Chapter 2 by turning to recent work on Higher Education by Dennis Hayes and other scholars working in the 'radical humanist' tradition in which *The Dangerous Rise of Therapeutic Education* is situated, including supporters of the Academics For Academic Freedom pressure group. I read in this a comparable contradiction to that introduced previously. Freedom of expression is deemed paramount, and respect is insisted upon, yet too much academic work is understood to be met with respect, and too many students and academics are allowed to express themselves. Such tensions inevitably arise, I would argue, in a text opposed to anything that threatens transparent communication within the transparent academic community. The gap must be closed, the opposition ejected and the university made pure once more through the sacrifice of the other that threatens what Bill Readings sardonically terms as the 'nature of the social bond', 'the object of free and rational assent in communication' (Readings 1996, p. 184).

In the final chapter, I address a text that defends the 'postmodernism' that Ecclestone and Hayes regard as the academic discourse of choice for the relativistic managerialism they seek to counter. Nigel Thrift's *Non-Representational Theory* argues against the kind of left-wing account of culture and society that understands capitalism only as a force that works against the interests of the oppressed. Although Thrift acknowledges there is a 'hard edge' to contemporary business practice, he sees also its potential for revolutionary change. It is claimed that the capitalist vanguard introduces opportunities for new understandings of what it means to be human: too often academics adopt the kind of human-centric philosophy supported by Ecclestone and Hayes, one premised on eternal truths and calcified identities. Thrift's vision, instead, is of a world in flux, where comforting and conservative ideas of human reality are challenged by the idea that, for example: the majority of what constitutes our experience occurs at a pre-cognitive level; objects in the world are as sentient as human subjects, and that we have come to exist as cyborgs, constituted by such objects; movement, feeling and physicality are of greater import than stability, thought and ideality. Thrift is particularly opposed to what he regards as an overtly linguistic and empirical approach to existence. Indeed, the very idea of 'meaning' is one that is understood to get in the way of the truth of the world: better to creatively engage 'the bare bones of actual occasions' (Thrift 2008, pp. 14, 2). Thrift's arguments are premised upon an absolute clarity of community and communication, even more so than that discussed in the preceding chapters. Indeed, in his view, 'signs act directly on the nervous system' (Thrift 2008, p. 115, quoting Marks). Language and cognition can be rejected, as they are not the site of experience; the actual is nothing to do with subjectivity but rests with physicality and the emotions. This is not, for Thrift, a materiality of certainty. It is temporal, and thus constantly changing and the objects within it are defined by the permeability of their borders. My suggestion, however, is that the authority of a prior real consistently stages a return to Thrift's argument. For Thrift, there is a material truth, no matter how complex and fluid that might be.

My concern in all this is the relation between *Non-Representational Theory* and new managerialism within the university. In arguing for the transparency of community, Thrift is particularly committed to the rejection of any discursive frame. For Thrift, a difficulty faces anyone wishing to call into question the material truth of the world as it is 'disclosed', as it is not, as indicated earlier, a matter of meaning. (Thrift 2008, p. 123) One cannot speak of it, as it is non-linguistic. If one thinks this truth might be something other than that 'disclosed', this is a matter of thinking only, and it is at another level, a level outside the restriction of the subject, that a genuine engagement with this truth is claimed to occur. Such engagement, however, is necessarily open to the scrutiny of the non-representational theorist. What I read in this is a repetition of the process of 'psychologisation' as identified recently by Jan de Vos, in which 'subjective' experience is understood in 'objective' terms. In this move, there is a claim to overcome the challenge of perspective, and thus also to offer up the truth of experience as available to all, despite this 'all' thereby exceeding its own experience: 'psychology's dictum *this is who you are* positions the subject not as the one he/she supposedly is, but as the one looking (as a proto-psychologist) at the one he/she supposedly is' (de Vos 2015, p. 252). Managerialism is also, I would argue, a discourse premised on the rejection of a constitutive frame. Its operation cannot be called into question. It is an understanding repeated in Chris Lorenz's claim that 'managerialism ... is totalitarian because it leaves no institutional room for criticism, which it always sees as subversion', and Thomas Docherty's insistence that:

> In the university, the authorized voice is that of the VC, whose HR function is to preside over the brand. To question that self-evident truth locates you in the realm of madness – or potentially, unemployment – because you are questioning the norm, the self-evident, the fundamental authority that believes that it needs no self-justification. (Lorenz 2012, p. 608; Docherty 2015, p. 135)

In this regard, it is significant that Nigel Thrift was until recently Vice-Chancellor at Warwick University, and a controversial figure while in this post, variously understood to encapsulate all that is wrong and right with the corporate university.[15] When I question what I take to be Thrift's authoritarian philosophy, I do so, therefore, in the context of his managerial role. I am interested in how Thrift's published academic work might be understood to relate to his position as Vice-Chancellor.

It seems to me that such an approach offers an opportunity for institutional critique at a time when dissent is limited. All those employed in Higher Education are working during a period of increased managerial control, one in which academics are concerned about speaking out against their employers: the cases of Ian Parker and Thomas Docherty indicate what can happen if academics refuse to tow the party line.[16] Even where such blatant managerial aggression is not in evidence, it is easy to see why those working within the university are reluctant to make public their opposition to university policy. Take, for example, the recent changes in contracts introduced by The University of Reading when updating its charter. As has been widely discussed in the media, a new clause has been inserted stating that staff are required to 'promote, protect and develop and extend the business and reputation of the university, its subsidiaries and its interests', and can be dismissed if they 'refuse or neglect to comply with any reasonable and lawful directions of the University' or act 'in any manner which, in the reasonable opinion of the University, is likely to bring the University or any subsidiary into disrepute or is materially adverse to the interests of the University or any subsidiary'.[17] University management has made it clear that 'staff are perfectly free, within the law, to question and test perceived wisdom and to put forward new ideas and controversial or unpopular opinions... There is a fundamental difference between academics being free to comment and bringing the institution into disrepute through fraudulent, dishonest or malicious behaviour'.[18] My concern here is that while this response can be read as a robust defence of academic freedom, the effect of public discussion of the ins-and-outs of summary dismissal is not likely to encourage dissenting voices. Thus, while I admire Gary Rolfe's decision in *The University in Dissent* to question his own university's practices, as 'critique, like charity, should begin at home', and I regard Derek Sayer's account of his time at Lancaster University in *Rank Hypocrisies* to be the most searing, inspiring and entertaining take on the problems within UK universities I have read, my own practice points in the opposite direction.[19] There are difficulties in addressing the relationship between the academic and administrative work of a VC from a university other than one's own: I know my own university well, and Warwick only vaguely; I have no interest in staging a personal attack; increasingly, VCs are not published academics. My interest, however, is in Docherty's notion of an '*authorized* voice' [my italics]. In my reading, Thrift's non-representational theory is limited by its inability to engage its own legitimizing authority: the truth of the world is 'disclosed' without any consideration of the positionality this demands, just as the culture of audit focuses on evidence rather the hearing of testimony. I understand my reading of the VC's texts to challenge the naturalization of authority across the university scene, a work of resistance that brings that which 'needs no self-justification' to discourse.

In all three chapters, my approach is to offer a sustained close reading of an individual text. There is a danger here: I realise that the result does not read like a conventional work on education, and I run the risk of my analysis being deemed partial, irrelevant or 'too esoteric'.[20] For me, this is a risk worth taking. I understand reading to call the certainty of the object and the transparency of meaning into question, requiring as it does a working through of the slippage of the signifier and the destabilising effects of perspective. A reading, moreover, cannot be assessed on its own terms from any position beyond itself without repeating that which it would contain. My method is not incidental to my meaning, in other words. Here I understand my work to engage a form of critique to which Bill Readings has cause to appeal within *The University in Ruins*: 'The late Paul de Man gave us the terms of a literary analysis that recognized the reading of literature as a necessary and impossible task; the same is true of the evaluation of the universities' (Readings 1996, p. 133). What, on these terms, would it mean to exclude sustained close reading from engagements with the university?

Objecthood is also challenged through my selection of texts. I realise that a two-decade old essay on sexual harassment, an account of bullying across the educational sector, and a philosophical work on affect are not the most obvious choices for staging a critique of Higher Education in the United Kingdom. Again, that, for me, is the point. In focusing on these texts, I open up the question of what might constitute an appropriate text for a discourse on the University: how might we trouble the limits of our object of study? And how might this in itself counter the discourse of audit?

Notes

1. I take the general formulation for the opening of this introduction from Martin, Ben. 2016. What is happening to our universities? *SWP Working Papers Series*. http://ssrn.com/abstract=2745139. Accessed 1 July 2016. My focus is on UK provision, and on the humanities. Fundamentally, this is because UK humanities provision is what I know. For a discussion of the difficulties of such a choice, see, of course, Readings (1996). See also the introduction to Sayer, Derek. 2015. *Rank hypocrisies: the insult of the REF*. London: Sage Swifts. As I make clear later, however, UK provision is located in a wider discourse of internationalisation and of globalisation. The limitless university is one that exceeds national borders. This does not mean that local social and economic differences cease to signify, but rather that they are often consigned to shadows cast by the illuminated university.
2. As Stefan Collini has it: 'we should register the subliminal capacity of the phrase "concrete achievement" to summon up disconcertingly apt images: there is something both pleasing and telling about the fantasy of responding to official requests to "justify" the humanities by having a series of dumper trucks deposit a huge pile of excellent scholarly books on the steps of the relevant ministry' Collini (2012), p. 85.
3. My appeal here is, for example, to Simon Morgan Wortham's suggestion that audit always requires a hearing. Wortham, Simon Morgan. 2006.

Counter-institutions: Jacques Derrida and the question of the University. New York: Fordham, p. 101.
4. In keeping with HEFCE's policy for Open Access, '[m]embers of the public can access bibliographic details and many refereed full text versions free of charge, for personal research or study, in accordance with our End User Agreement'. University of Reading. http://centaur.reading.ac.uk/. Accessed 18 August 2016. I should add here that I am a supporter of Open Access.
5. See, for example, the email policy of Aberystwyth University: 'Monitoring [of email] means that all or part of an email is inspected either automatically or by nominated University officers without further seeking your permission.... University staff never routinely inspect the contents of any e-mail. However, in accordance with the Regulation of Investigatory Powers Act 2000, there are occasions where some or all of this information may be viewed...Where the Pro Vice-Chancellor (Student and Staff Services), or, in his/her absence, the Director of Information Services or the Director of Human Resources, believes there is a *prima facie* suspicion that the University's Regulations or Policy on the use of e-mail have been contravened'. Furthermore: 'You must not send e-mail messages that show the University in an unprofessional light or that could expose the University to legal liability. E-mails sent by a member of the University have the same standing as a letter on headed notepaper even if you describe the contents as "private". If you wish to send e-mail and not be bound by this undertaking you should use an external e-mail provider'. University of Aberystwyth. Policies. http://www.aber.ac.uk/en/infocompliance/policies/e-mail/. Accessed 21 August 2016.
6. All emails are understood to be the property of the university, see, for example, 'all@port.ac.uk email addresses, associated accounts and work-related emails are the property of the University'. University of Portsmouth. http://policies.docstore.port.ac.uk/policy-070.pdf (2016). As many universities increasingly act against unauthorised transmission of material relating to its activities, especially, as we shall see, when it regards these as being against its interests, the move to publish emails in a book such as this would meet with institutional resistance.
7. This contention can be read in texts from very different political standpoints. Clive Kessler makes the familiar case when claiming that the 'neo-liberal ascendancy had to undermine the structures of intellectual authority that resided within the established disciplines. To prevail it had to disarm the capacity for effective intellectual critique they threatened to offer'. Kessler, Clive. 2010. Between a postmodernist and a hard place. *The Australian.* http://www.theaustralian.com.au/higher-education/between-a-postmodernist-and-a-hard-case/story-e6frgcjx-1225877158821. Accessed 18 August 2016. See also Saunders, Malcom. 1996. The madness and malady of managerialism.

Quadrant 50/3: 9–17. For recent examples see Sanbonmatsu, John. 2015. Postmodernism and the corruption of the critical intelligentsia. In *Radical intellectuals and the subversion of progressive politics: The betrayal of politics*, eds. Michael J. Thompson, and Gregory Smulewicz-Zucker. New York: Palgrave Macmillan; Ecclestone and Hayes (2009), as discussed in Chapter 2 of this present book. See Collini (2012), for what I take to be a particularly clear critique of post-modernity within Higher Education discourse.
8. See also Shore, Cris. 2008. Audit culture and illiberal governance: Universities and the culture of accountability. *Anthropological Theory* 8: 278–298.
9. See also Docherty (2015), p. 123.
10. See Štech, Stanislav. 2012. The Bologna process as a new public management tool in higher education. *Journal of Pedagogy* 2/2: 263–282; Ward, Steven. 2012. *Neoliberalism and the global restructuring of knowledge and education*. New York: Routledge; 2014. Araya, Daniel and Marber, Peter, eds. *Higher Education in the global Age: Policy, practice and promise in emerging societies*. Abingdon: Routledge; Lorenz (2012), pp. 599–629.
11. Von Osten, Marion. 2011. Education reforms in a European context. In *The assault on universities: A manifesto for resistance*, eds. Michael Bailey and Des Freedman, 157–167. London: PlutoPress.
12. For this, see Readings (1996), p. 134: 'Judgement is better understood in relation to a continuing *discussion* rather than as a finality. To whom and to what the University remains accountable are questions we must continue to pose and worry over. Appeals to accounting – whether in the form of numerically scored teaching evaluations, efficiency ratings, or other bureaucratic statistics – will only serve to prop up the logic of consumerism that rules the University of Excellence. Value is a question of judgement, a question whose answers must be continually discussed.'
13. For a critique of the supplement, see Readings (1996), p. 124: 'we need no new identity for the University, not even the supplement will save us'. I am interested, rather, in Simon Morgan Wortham's contention 'that today's "audit culture" tries its best to minimize testimony at the expense of evidence' yet '"evidence" can never be pure of, can never simply take leave of, testimony', Wortham (2006), pp. 101–103.
14. Ecclestone and Hayes (2009), p. xiii.
15. For more on this, see Chapter 3.
16. Legge, James. 2012. Manchester Metropolitan: 'Bullying' university bans world-renowned professor who spoke out. *The Independent*, October 24; Morgan, John. 2014. Thomas Docherty 'to be cleared of all charges' by Warwick. *Times Higher Education*, October 21.
17. Quoted in Grove, Jack. 2016. Reading lecturers rebel over 'erosion of academic freedom' in new contracts. *Times Higher Education Supplement*,

August 6. The University stresses that the alterations are an exercise in 'modernising and strengthening our charter', this helping to maintain all academic freedoms. See University of Reading. https://www.reading.ac.uk/charter-reform/cr-home.aspx. Accessed 1 September 2016.
18. Quoted in Grove (2016).
19. Rolfe, Gary. 2013. *The university in dissent: Scholarship in the corporate university*. London: Palgrave, p. 54; Sayer (2015).
20. This from a conversation between myself and an academic who publishes questioning, historically situated critiques of the neo-liberal university.

References

Ball, Stephan. 1994. *Education reform: A critical and post-structural approach*. Buckingham: Open University Press.

Collini, Stefan. 2012. *What are universities for?* London: Penguin.

De Vos, Jan. Self-help and pop-psychology. In *Handbook of critical psychology*, ed. Ian Parker, 250–258. London: Routledge.

Docherty, Thomas. 2015. *Universities at war*. London: Sage Swifts.

Ecclestone, Kathryn and Dennis Hayes. 2009. *The dangerous rise in therapeutic education*. London: Routledge.

House, Richard. 2014. Reimagining the university – an urgent cultural and paradigmatic Imperative. http://www.criticalinstitute.org/re-imagining-university/. Accessed 1 July 2016.

Lorenz, Chris. 2012. If you're so smart, why are you under surveillance? Universities, neoliberalism, and New Public Management. *Critical Inquiry* 38: 599–629.

Purkiss, Diane. 1994. The lecherous professor revisited: Plato, pedagogy and the scene of harassment. In *Rethinking sexual harassment*, eds. Clare Brant and Yun Lee Too, 187–219. London: Sage.

Readings, Bill. 1996. *The university in ruins*. Cambridge, MA, and London: Harvard University Press.

Thrift, Nigel. 2008. *Non-representational theory: Space/politics/affect*. London: Routledge.

Wortham, Simon Morgan. 2006. *Counter-institutions: Jacques Derrida and the question of the University*. New York: Fordham.

CHAPTER 2

'[…] Not much like a Grove […]': Openness, Object, and *Agora* in 'The Lecherous Professor Revisited' by Diane Purkiss

Abstract This chapter analyses a text that makes an urgent case for the primacy of the object within university pedagogy, and for commercial education: 'The Lecherous Professor Revisited' by Diane Purkiss (The lecherous professor revisited: Plato, pedagogy and the scene of harassment, Sage, London; 1994). Purkiss considers contemporary university teaching a 'harasser's charter', the tentative solution to which is a more visible, public form of pedagogy. Taking her cue from the Athenian agora, Purkiss imagines an open, digitized space, where students move freely, having no intense relationships with lecturers. This vision can be understood to have been subsequently realized within new-managerialist provision. If Purkiss recognizes commercialised education as dangerous, it is a danger that has no bearing on the object. The commitment is to 'transparent' communication and community, for Bill Readings the defining features of 'The University of Excellence'.

Keywords Diane Purkiss · Openness · Pharmakon

1 Introduction

In this second chapter, I am interested in working through a tension within Higher Education debates concerned with humanities provision and the question of 'openness'. One established response to an ever more pervasive audit culture, with its demand for the university to justify itself in its every instance, is to insist on subject specialism and the necessity of faculty, the good of which is bound to knowledge not easily translatable in general terms: we are necessary because we are experts. One disadvantage of such a move is the support it can offer discourses of elitism and obscurity, a privileging of exclusive authority.[1] To thoroughly counter such a position, the humanities are encouraged to be more open, their worth now situated in their inclusivity, their potential for enabling democracy. Yet this is to stray into the very territory staked out by new managerialism: the thoroughly accessible, universally applicable, realm of the audit. It is a difficulty recently identified, for example, by Martin Paul Eve when discussing the contemporary academic publishing scene in his *Open Access and the Humanities*: 'If open access is adopted [isolationism can be] mitigated where desirable, but sometimes at the price of playing into a justification on the basis of transparency and appraisal, qualification and measurement, among the many other controversies' (Eve 2014, p. 55).

In what follows, I will work through the risk of openness suggested here from what might seem a somewhat unlikely starting point: a 22-year-old study of sexual ethics. I have chosen to engage 'The Lecherous Professor Revisited' by Diane Purkiss precisely because it can help to question the category of new managerialism.[2] This chapter, from a collection addressing issues of sexual harassment within a range of institutions, could be understood to oppose new managerial discourses or, at the very least, fall outside their bounds: the work was published in 1993, prior to the emergence of the Blairite 'neo-technocratic managerialism', while conversely, its commitment to a working through of sexual ethics sets it apart from forms of managerialism that are motivated solely by issues of profit and self-replication.[3] As I will argue in detail later, I take this text to offer a rigorous critique of patriarchal pedagogy, especially, although not exclusively that, experienced within Oxford University in the early 1990s, one characterised by its failure to own up and publically discuss its privileges and demands. According to Purkiss, this inability of the institution to reflect upon its own gendered positionality is not only announced through its attitudes to sexual harassment, but also in the way it structures teaching and assessment. Although I wholly agree with this diagnosis, I remain unconvinced by a further contention that solutions are to be found in market-based provision. Rather, I understand the scene of learning that is promoted within 'The Lecherous Professor Revisited', with its interest in a customer-focused, digitized and commercial education, focused upon skills, and delivered by a roster of academics granted no overall responsibility for modules, to be comparable to that taken up within new managerial discourse. This can, after all, be compared to the pedagogical situation famously critiqued by John Henry Newman: 'a sort of bazaar, or pantechnicon, in which wares of all kinds are heaped together in stalls independent of each other'.[4] In David Noble's comparably classic formulation, what is being supported is an approach to learning founded on the 'disintegration and distillation of the educational experience into discrete, reified and ultimately saleable things or packages of things' (Noble 2001, p. 3). On these terms, I would argue a further connection to Purkiss's text can be made. Just as managerialism's investment in 'things' always requires a failure to recognise the excess through which they are constituted, its audit taking no account of the necessity of hearing, and in any case, 'barely reflect[ing] what actually takes place in the educational experience', so 'The Lecherous Professor Revisited' understands the good of education to rest within the object, divested of supplement (Noble 2001, p. 3). The advantage of the marketplace, for Purkiss, is that within it all is out in the open, and it is this that will limit the power of an obscurest and unreflective patriarchy. 'The Lecherous Professor Revisited' thus shares with such foundational supporters of Blairite new managerialism as Michael Barber, the belief that a pedagogy premised on the hidden and hierarchical can be countered by 'the power of choice [and] transparency'.[5] In one sense, therefore, what we are reading here is simply a foreshadowing of 'neo-technocratic managerialism', with its commitment to 'co-production' and 'empowerment', its faith in the openness of audit as an enabler of institutional reform.[6]

One difficulty for 'The Lecherous Professor Revisited' in this is that with hindsight, Noble's critique of the institutional, commercial and repressive can be understood to have become only more relevant and damning in the wake of such reforms. Here, for example, is Bronwyn Davies's formulation of the problem as it relates to the position of women within the university:

> One of [the] cleverest, and perhaps the most devious, strategies of new managerialism has been the inclusion of equity discourses in the objectives that institutions were impelled to include. Many feminists were drawn into managerialism – and so into the new *episteme* – in which their professional life was reconstituted in the terms of auditors and economists because of their desire for change. It seemed to offer an alternative to the old hierarchies of power and control. (Davies 2003, p. 95)

Whether or not one is to go along with the notion of an explicit intent to deceive, the force of this argument remains: for some, new-managerialism was understood to offer a way out of an existing, repressive and patriarchal structure. Purkiss makes a strong case for understanding the contemporary situation within Higher Education as intolerable, and thus also for the necessity of moving forward (Purkiss 1994, pp. 207–208). Although difficulties are recognised in this course of action, a certain public, open, illuminated and commercial form of provision is understood to offer a way out (Purkiss 1994, pp. 215–218). Again, as I will discuss in more detail in the following section, it is possible now to claim that those who heeded the managerial call were not directed to a liberated space, but one of regulation and control (Davies 2003, p. 176). In Davies's estimation, the audit culture 'has not made the university more egalitarian', but more aggressive, less happy to celebrate difference, or to address the ways in which the experience of work can be constituted by gender.[7] Indeed, for Thomas Docherty, the irony is that, counter to the predictions made within 'The Lecherous Professor Revisited', reforming new managerial approaches have not brought the hidden to light, but instead have cast their own kind of darkness, resulting in the obscure returning as a site of resistance, rather than repression:

> The Official University – the transparent one, replete with information – has not only eviscerated, but also threatened with extinction those elements in the institution where the serious work – research and teaching – goes on. The institution, if it is to survive, has to become clandestine, existing in the 'shadowy terrain' in the interstices of officialdom. (Docherty 2015, p. 122)

Managerialism within 'The Official University' cannot tolerate anything that might be beyond its power, which might resist the openness, consistency and legibility required by a global, commercial and inter-disciplinary institution. In Bill Reading's celebrated formulation, as discussed in the introduction to this present book, this is the logic of 'the University of Excellence, where excellence names a non-referential principle that allows the maximum of uninterrupted internal administration' (Readings 1996, p. 120). Indeed, as also suggested earlier, the 'efficiency' of 'excellence' ultimately requires even the institutional border to be traversed, as evidenced by the trans-national Bologna Accords, a globalizing structure that 'moves to standardize all of higher education in terms of interchangeable modules', a 'deterritorializ[ing]' move that relocates cultural and economic difference to a 'clandestine' space (Lorenz 2012, p. 612).[8]

In what follows, I am interested in the extent to which Docherty's argument opens up the possibility that even the most well-intentioned drive to transparency might, of necessity, produce a shadow. Confronted by the obscurity that privilege requires and creates, it is easy to sympathise with a response that demands everything be put on show. After all, to quote Readings again, for 'the majority of left-wing critics' of the University, 'all that is needed to set things right is clearer (true) communication: the truth will set us free' (Readings 1996, p. 183). The danger is that the realisation of such a demand might lead not to an institution shorn of supplement, but one that must repress the excess of labour and meaning upon which it calls.

2   Seminar Absence

'The Lecherous Professor Revisited' opens its argument with the claim that problems within contemporary Higher Education provision can be read out from the very term 'The Lecherous Professor', this the title of a previous publication addressing the issue of sexual harassment on campus.[9] Purkiss works through the various possibilities of the term, including the sense in which it allows the separation of personal ethics and professional identity. There is nothing lecherous about professorship in general, so the established discourse asserts, it is only that this or that particular professor happens to be in this condition. In this way, issues of gender and sexuality can be constituted as private matters, and as such, there is apparently no need for institutional reflection. Traditional divisions between teaching and research come into play here, as professional identity tends to be identified exclusively with the latter. This places teaching in the realm of the private, this, suggests Purkiss, the reason for the dearth of academics addressing their own teaching practice within publications. Teaching is thus, worryingly unregulated, invisible to the institution, meaning that male academics find that their sexuality and their teaching occupy the same, occulted space. It is in this sense that the contemporary educational structure acts as 'a harasser's charter' (Purkiss 1994, p. 210). 'The Lecherous Professor Revisited' is interested in making visible this aspect of institutional life, opening up and politicising not only claims to 'personal' sexuality, but also the structures that govern classroom and assessment practice.[10]

Purkiss's initial objection to contemporary assessment and teaching is that it fails to deliver on its promise. Despite claiming to promote freedom and equality, in practice, it is hierarchical and restraining. This is reflective of the kind of silence and invisibility that is understood to be the enabling condition of patriarchy within the institution. Essay assessment, for example, depends upon 'hazy but holy criteria for "quality"' that 'are never discussed or examined systematically' (Purkiss 1994, p. 194). The form of the essay is questionable, on the other hand, because it 'requires a rhetoric of dogmatic certainty', a 'production of smoothness, evenness and narrowness rather than range, diversity and eclecticism. The goal is tight control rather than wide interest' (Purkiss 1994, p. 194). Here, I would contend, something of the constitutive tensions between clarity and obscurity within Purkiss's argument that I will be addressing later can be read: the rules that govern assessment are taken to be problematic because they can never be announced, yet its products are only too certain.

In a sense, seminars are also understood to suffer from a lack of 'range', as they '[depend] crucially on the notional egalitarianism of shared reading', that is the 'specious but useful fantasy' that 'the photocopied article is a level playing field', that 'by all reading [Frederick] Jameson, we are somehow all alike; even if in practice we read it differently' (Purkiss 1994, p. 195). Although it would appear that, within the singular, undifferentiated field, all have an equivalent opportunity to demonstrate their interpretive skill, the tutor, unlike the student, has 'not only read that one piece by Jameson several times, but also several of Jameson's books, accounts of Jameson by other theorists and the work of at least some of the theorists whom Jameson sites or rewrites' (Purkiss 1994, p. 195). The tutor is therefore in a 'privileged position in relation' to the text, and their task is to 'transmit that privilege' (Purkiss 1994, p. 195). In other words, as a tutor, 'I am trying to make students resemble me, resemble or mimic my mastery of Jameson' (Purkiss 1994, p. 195). This is understood even to be the case when students disagree with a lecturer's interpretation of the text in question, as this merely demonstrates the successful mimicry of mastery: 'acts of disagreement do not escape the imitation game or its logic' (Purkiss 1994, p. 196). It is worth thinking a little, at this stage, about the precise terms in which reading is constructed within this argument. It is not, for example, understood as dynamic or surprising, and there is seemingly no need to address the specifics of any particular textual encounter. Instead, the focus is on the lecturer's engagement with other texts, and how this bestows a position of authority. Fundamental to the idea of position is that it can be taken up by another.[11] Purkiss is aware of the danger in such a formulation, as mimicry, in one sense, can be reactionary, and thus a cause for concern, without falling into slavish repetition. Thus, for example, students can take on the position of mastery in a casual way, leaving it at the door; a power dynamic still divides students from teachers; mimicry does not mean a wholesale copy; as suggested previously, one can argue against the lecturer and still mimic him (Purkiss 1994, p. 197). I would suggest, however, that a problematic commitment to a limited repetition remains:

> The fact is that within a seminar there *are* unwritten and unexamined rules about what counts as valid; the object of going to the seminar is indeed in part to learn these rules. The rules are administered by the tutor, and the first rule is that students must imitate the tutor ['students are supposed to imitate my mastery of Jameson']. (Purkiss 1994, p. 196)

Despite the designated roles within the process of imitation, positionality is not rooted in the instance; it does not matter whether the subject is student or tutor, one reading or another, a temporary role or permanent identity. The problem that taxes Purkiss is that of a conservative passing on of the same; an unquestioned, unchanging and excluding privilege. For this to be the case, however, at this stage at least, the site of truth is not to be that of writing, but a form that is both beyond and within. It is, to borrow a formulation from Paul de Man, as if writing is to be approached only through 'extra-linguistic generalisation', with analysis rooted in 'observations that could be paraphrased or translated in terms of common knowledge' (De Man 1982, p. 9). Initially, as read earlier, the problem with assessment, as formulated within 'The Lecherous Professor Revisited', is that it is dependent upon the unannounced, and, therefore, the 'hazy'. Here, there is nothing 'hazy' about the unwritten law. The issue, for Purkiss, is that in being hidden it is positioned in the space of the harasser, removed from public scrutiny; yet, there is no doubt that it waits to be 'administered', and equally there is no doubt as to what it is, whatever form it might choose to take. Within this pedagogical scene, what is bequeathed is not a chain of reading, impossible to finally stand beyond, but a stable, unwritten form.

3   Stall Holders and S-Bends

If a subtle move away from the textual can be read in Purkiss's account of the seminar, it is one that, I would argue, becomes more pronounced in what might be considered the main scene of 'The Lecherous Professor Revisited': the vision of a liberated, object-centred education with which its argument closes. Essentially, the idea is that the university should relocate from a private, cloistered environment to an open market, a place where clarity and accessibility will limit the power of patriarchy to replicate itself through invisibility and repression. Even at this early stage difficulties may be read. Certainly, escaping the enclosed space can only help to widen participation, but in one sense this move is nevertheless premised on exclusion. What must be set aside for the limitless market in education to flourish? Here, I am not interested in defending the place of privilege, but rather arguing that openness, in whatever way understood, requires something, at least, to be closed, for good or ill.

I would suggest that the challenge of squaring ideas of difference and division can also be read in Purkiss's initial appeal to the work of Gargi Bhattacharyya: considering that 'universities have spent a lot of energy in defensive rhetoric, fictively claiming to preserve a separation from the marketplace which does not really exist', might we not ask 'whether closing the gap between academe and the *agora* might offer something to us'? (Purkiss 1994, p. 210). An initial difficulty here is that, if separations between university and marketplace, or rhetoric and action, are fictive, there is an issue with the idea that they can be 'clos[ed]'. I read this only to become more problematic with the subsequent explanation:

> [i]f we left the pastoral groves of academe and instead reconfigured them as the open *agora*, a space of buying and selling and yelling, a public space, would eroticised insemination still be the hidden motivator of all our actions? The Platonic model is conceptually dependent on spatial location; we don't assume any transcendent transference between shop assistants and their merchandise, or between plumbers and the S-bend. (Purkiss 1994, p. 210)

Although there is little doubt at this point that we do really leave the pastoral grove, it could be argued that the mundane reality of the separation is questioned, as 'the open *agora*' is a figurative space, and thus not necessarily a discrete, unchanging 'real'. A problem remains, however, as what is being reconfigured is a 'them': 'pastoral groves'. If this frames 'pastoral groves' as the real, recoverable even in their figuration as something else, it also opens a fundamental difficulty: how can the border between *agora* and grove be adequately policed if the one can indeed be figured as the other?

To further interrogate the notion of repetition and replacement on offer, it is worth looking in more detail at the precise terms in which the *agora* is constructed: as a 'space', one 'of' action, 'of buying and selling and yelling'. It is thus a 'space' that can be understood to oppose the 'rhetorical', as discussed earlier. 'Yelling', after all, is not quite speaking. It confirms the public nature of the 'space'.[12] Yelling, thus constructed, is contentless. This can be understood to be a necessity, as if instanced, the yell would have meaning, and thus, division. In this way, the very openness of the yell, its apparent linguistic indivisibilty, can return as lack. Within the space of the *agora*, openness can be figured as an absence.

It is an opposition that can be read to be destabilised elsewhere within the quotation concerning 'the pastoral groves of academe'. Take the space beyond the *agora*, necessary always to its figuration. There the threat is that of the occulted, with 'eroticised insemination' problematically 'the hidden motivator of all our actions'. It is crucial for this argument that eroticised insemination is other than action, yet it can also be read as an active cause, this suggesting that prior to 'all' action is another action. In any case, the 'hidden motivator' throws up issues of perspective: the narration somehow knows what our actions mean to us, a knowledge to which we have no access: action is supremely translatable, suffering no limit. It is a reading of action that can be further problematised if we return to 'yelling', which I take to be an action, yet, in this formulation, one that changes the nature of action. 'All' actions are motivated by erotic insemination, yet it is action, within the reconfigured pastoral groves of academe that is the open *agora* that secures the openness located there, and releases all actions from their hidden motivation: the erotic insemination that is not action.

What is challenged in all of this, I would suggest, is an investment in the indivisible essence, necessary to a discourse of openness. It is an investment to be read, for example, in the notion that within the figure of the open *agora*, we do not expect people to have any kind of special relationship to what their job ties them to, the lack of any sense of 'insemination' as a 'transcendent transference'. In the absence of such transcendence, which I read here in terms of a higher or another purpose, an 'S-bend' *is simply itself*. This is the enabling condition of open education. What must be repressed in this is the extent to which, in its construction of the *agora*, 'The Lecherous Professor Revisited' requires, for example, 'action', to be thoroughly turned against itself: the *agora* is not so much the container of crystalline, self-present objects, as the difference necessary to meaning. Counter to this, the realm of the hidden that should stand in a position opposed to the self- sufficient identity of the market is constituted in terms of a motivation that is fully accessible and unchanging. As also read in the account of patriarchal replication earlier, the hidden is 'unwritten' and predictable, the site of what I take to be an 'intact' transmission.

'The Lecherous Professor Revisited' confirms and develops its commitment to the object in the following construction of the *agora* as:

> a noisy, public place in which professorship means being both maker and a stallholder. We should represent seminars, tutorials and symposia as workshops, in which professors and students alike work to shape a variety of commodities, of which the student might be *one*. This does not have to imply a careless, dehumanising transaction if we think of ourselves and our students *together* occupying the place of crafter, shaping the object of the craft to the highest possible smoothness and gloss. (Purkiss 1994, pp. 210–211)

Although, once again, there is resistance to a discourse of naïve materialism, with the representative nature of what is being discussed explicitly addressed, the claim here is for an education centred on the object. As already can be read in the appeal to the 'S-bend' mentioned earlier, education, figured as transaction, is not taken to be transcendental, but something localised and present. In the initial quotation, however, the understanding of plumbing as lacking any constitutive excess is narrated from a position outside the transference it rejects, and it would seem nothing needs to be added to this exteriorised knowledge. In the desired form of education, located in the *agora*, the self-sufficiency of the relation is repeated, and thus there is something there that is equivalent to both 'S-bend' and 'merchandise'. This is a reading of education as functional; intentional labour results in 'the object of the craft' being shaped in a particular way. There is no interest in anything extraneous to the process. Constructing educational work in this way means that the question of language is also removed from consideration, and it should be remembered that this idea of teaching stands in opposition to that focused on the 'specious fantasy' of a collective reading of the photocopied sheet. To engage in such work, outside questions of writing, is understood to be possibly 'humanising', and that is, in part, because of the 'care' that goes into it. The care tempers the danger: unlike the pedagogy of harassment, this does not rest on careless, hidden assumptions. Despite this, it is an education that asks the student, at one stage, to take the place vacated by the S-bend. Purkiss claims that we should be 'aiming together to produce a good, marketable, valuable commodity' as this is what students 'expect of us'; yet this entails a marketable student, whose good is bound to its status as commodity (Purkiss 1994, p. 211).[13]

'The Lecherous Professor Revisited' is aware of the risk inherent in these formulations, the threat of misogynistic and reductive re-appropriation: 'I can see only too clearly how many [of these ideas] could be adapted to the maintenance of the existing state of affairs', reliant as they are upon notions of 'women as sexual commodities' and 'Gradgrindian forms of classroom oppression' (Purkiss 1994, p. 213). This caution as to the object is significant, yet, I would maintain, limited. The understandable focus on the objectification of women and the oppressive nature of rote learning does not situate the pedagogical problem as one of clarity. Bronwyn Davies, for example, sees the discourse of 'auditor' and 'equity' within which this kind of open, illuminated learning is promoted, to have further implications for feminist academics, as it tends to favour:

> a much tougher, more 'macho' kind of academic, and encourage a climate where due process, equity, and respect for academic freedom are overwhelmed by the need to respond quickly to opportunities, reinvent, repackage and position oneself and one's institution in the marketplace. (Davies 2003, p. 176, quoting Johanna Wyn)

Davies further contends that as the focus on accountability and consumer demand requires the institution to 'get more for less staff', workloads increase and there is competition for ever-reduced resources, this in an environment that does not encourage open discussion or the established checks that help counter repressive policy. Certainly there are men and women who thrive within this structure, but equally there are ways of working that are not encouraged. Market forces mean that 'some kinds of teaching – and knowledge – are given priority', and feminist courses have often been amongst those deleted from the books.[14] Moreover, as the faith in information technology privileges 'modulated, unitised, pre-packaged kinds of teaching', the kind of questioning work that characterises feminist study is not encouraged (Davies 2003, pp. 176–177).[15]

The issue then, is that the public nature of the market does not guarantee its status as a fresh or collectively held space. David Noble's description of innovations within American Higher Education in the 1990s, especially those that, like Purkiss's *agora*, focus on the democratising potential of new technology, can be understood to sound a warning here:

> At the expense of the original integrity of the educational process, instruction has ... been transformed into a set of deliverable commodities ... In the

wake of this transformation, teachers become commodity producers and deliverers, subject to the familiar regime of commodity production in any other industry, and students become consumers of yet more commodities. (Noble 2001, pp. 3–4)[16]

For Noble, repression within commercialised education is less a risk than an inevitability. To enter the market is not to find oneself in a levelled out space of possibility, but subject, instead, to an established 'regime'. Although a narrative of self-replication might be read as returning to Noble's formulation, my interest is with his suggestion that any negotiable identity is to be caught within the discourse of commodity.[17] In my analysis, even as the argument of 'The Lecherous Professor Revisited' aims to 'disrupt paternalism and question the workings of authority' in its model of preferred education, at certain stages it fetishises authority in the object, abstracted from constitutive structures of relation, working within a framework that is committed to the seemingly 'level playing field' of the free market (Purkiss 1994, p. 212), or put another way, the scene of working class labour within the *agora*, as 'assumed' by another, is morally pure for precisely the reasons that the established pedagogical relationship is suspect: both are formed in a rejection of the supplement; an avoidance of wider, formative structures, with 'the milieu... not analysed and hence not blamed' (Purkiss 1994, p. 191).

It is my suggestion that this tension between the good object and the bad, as read earlier, is played out elsewhere within 'The Lecherous Professor Revisited': although we read that the goal of education is to produce a craft object of the 'highest possible smoothness and gloss', the most problematic form of assessment is one that requires the 'production of smoothness, evenness and narrowness rather than range' (Purkiss 1994, p. 211). Smoothness promises objecthood without difference, and thus protects against the absence upon which patriarchy is predicated; yet, it is also a sign of reductive practice, a denial of the difference that patriarchy would repress.

Here I think a connection can be made to 'Plato's Pharmacy', Jacques Derrida's account of writing and inheritance in *Phaedrus*, discussed at length in 'The Lecherous Professor Revisited'. Purkiss reads this work as a critique of 'erotic insemination', the patriarchal myth of self-replication and 'intact' transmission that informs provision at Oxford University (Purkiss 1994, p. 202). 'Plato's Pharmacy' is interested in the difficulty of 'sons', 'fathers', 'semen' and 'words' ever being delimited and discrete participants in exchange, visible to us for what they seemingly are.

Instead, it is claimed, they enter this dynamic only through an enabling structure of difference – a writing – that Derrida identifies as *pharmakon*, a word meaning, at the very least, both poison and cure. There is, for Derrida, a primary division in meaning that can never be traced back to a single point of origin, and thus is never available to us *as is*. As such, the *pharmakon* is an affront to 'the proper order and healthy movement of goods', that 'philosophical, dialectical mastery... that should be handed down from legitimate father to well-born son' (Derrida 2012, p. 168). As Purkiss has it: '[w]riting gets between teacher and pupil, or between father and son, breaking the ties of paternal self-replication and filial obedience which ensure the passage of truth from one generation to the next' (Purkiss 1994, p. 202). From my aforementioned reading, however, I would suggest that the *pharmakon* does not keep to its 'right' place within 'The Lecherous Professor Revisited', disrupting the stability of category required within the *agora* as much as the familial iterations of inheritance. I understand 'smoothness' within Purkiss's argument as *pharmakon*, both poison and cure. Smoothness fails to stand against the occult practices of patriarchy as much through its objecthood as its superficiality.

For an additional example, one might contrast the quotation introduced previously advocating the representation of 'symposia as workshops, in which the professor and students alike work to shape various commodities, of which the student might be *one*', with the claim that within a certain 'dreadful' kind of 'feminised' provision students are understood to be 'raw material like PlayDoh' (Purkiss 1994, p. 209). If 'management speakers' 'shap[ing]' 'raw material' in an 'underpaid, undervalued and feminised space of teaching' constitutes a problem, it is one repeated in the solution, focused as it is upon the 'shaping' of 'commodities' (Purkiss 1994, p. 209). Here, in the only instance of the managerial discussed within 'The Lecherous Professor Revisited', a distinction is made between it and the space of the *agora*, yet the very stuff of distinction – the act of 'shaping' and the material shaped – is collectively held.

In my reading, 'The Lecherous Professor Revisited', in its construction of the open place of education, is unable to read through the *pharmakon*. No matter whether it is critiquing the worst kind of education, or defining the best, it requires an indivisible object. This object is, however, necessarily divided: it is the 'myth' of semen within *Phaedrus* and the non-neurotic object, wonderfully divested of transference and desire.

Crucially, the notion of *pharmakon* also brings into question the analogies upon which 'The Lecherous Professor Revisited' relies. The understanding is that a range of individual, discrete identities are open for exchange: the 'pastoral glade' figured as *agora*; the student standing in for the S-bend. The idea, I think, is that this is a matter of difference, with each of these, of necessity, available as itself. What we have instead, I would argue, is *différance*, with the student assured of its stability and objecthood through its ability to be replaced by an 'S-bend'. Within a retrospective formation, this operation produces 'the student' already as the commodity; that is now, fundamentally, *what it is*. For this reason the student is always, in its primal condition, divided from itself. It is what it is not, and as such, it can never be fully open to vision. I would suggest it is in this textual movement of deferral, rather than in what Purkiss identifies elsewhere as a discrete set of 'metaphors and myths', that writing can be read to get 'between teacher and pupil, or between father and son, breaking the ties of filial obedience' (Purkiss 1994, p. 202).

Purkiss's vision of a public, democratic pedagogical space must, as I have argued, resist such difficulties. Education in the *agora* is understood to be open and democratic in so far as it is supremely translatable; translatable precisely because it is premised upon the object. It does not get mired in the sexual, the invisible, the excessive, or the linguistic. It is the kind of radicalism that Bill Reading reads in Claude Allègre's account of the 1968 protests, understood as 'opening up a university that was folded in on itself and bringing it closer to the city', this forming the basis for an appeal to 'integration' and 'excellence', the result of which is the fully transparent and mobile university, free from difference, and capable of smooth administration (Readings 1996, p. 36).

Here David Noble's focus on new technology in his criticism of the educational marketplace is telling, as, in keeping with suggestions made within 'The Lecherous Professor Revisited', it is in contemporary digitized provision that the appeals to the transparent and translatable are at their most insistent. Examples are legion, but we might begin with Richard House's insight that '[p]ractices like posting up lecture notes to students before lectures and compulsory PowerPoints in lectures' offer clarity and openness at the price of making original thinking impossible. For House, such practices rely upon 'learning outcomes' through which '[t]he creative space of not-knowing from which new, living thinking can emerge... is being... attenuated... the specification of what students are going to learn prior to the learning experience itself is in grave danger of yielding little more than learning that can only reinforce and buttress status-quo thinking' (House 2014). For an additional example, one could turn to the international success of the 'Visible Classroom' project, and its interest in using technology to help teacher's 'regularly evaluate their impact in their classroom and adjust their teaching methodology in response to what they see'. The claim is that the 'classroom needs to be made visible', with technology companies such as AI Media helping the process of 'seeing clearly what teachers are teaching and what students are learning'. One part of the project claims to secure clarity of understanding for Autism Spectrum Disorder students through lecture captions that 'take out figurative language' (AI Media 2014; Visible Classroom 2015).[18] The suggestion is that ideas are capable of being reduced to a non-figurative level, a translation that, I would suggest, opens up the possibility of commodification. It is a move I read also within TED Talks, an educational venture that can be understood to realise many of Purkiss's ideas for the future of pedagogy, while also suggesting the universalizing direction in which much digital teaching within Higher Education is heading. Participants are encouraged to share ideas with as much 'clarity' as possible in 17 minute, uni-directional lectures, these free to anyone with an internet connection.[19] Although there is no collaboration, we do have the lecturer as sole trader, behind his or her 'booth', everything out in the open, and no one staying around long enough for any hidden structure of insemination to be realised. In my reading this is a perfect expression of education as product, as 'S-bend'. Crucially here it is the progressive aspect of TED Talks, its very commitment to transparency and not-for-profit, democratic access, that opens up the place of the limitless university, and in this, as I will now elaborate, calls upon its double, that framed as the dangerous, reductive and compliant pedagogy of 'smoothness'.

4   Conclusion: Sacrifice and *Agora*

To conclude, then, I wish to think a little more about the strange, constitutive divisions of the *pharmakon*, and as such I find it helpful to return, briefly, to the spatial division that is of such importance to the separation of desired and derided forms of education within 'The Lecherous Professor Revisited'. For Purkiss:

> The parkland signifies the academy's separation from the public spaces of *polis* and *agora*. This design is testimony to a vision of the university as an enclosed world which replicates but also draws itself away from the public world of the *polis*. (Purkiss 1994, p. 198)

This vision of the established University is understood to attempt a separation from the *polis*, and in this falls into repetition. The result is a space both public and enclosed. Counter to this, the pedagogical scene that is to be promoted in 'The Lecherous Professor Revisited' is one that moves to overcome such distance. It is less turned upon itself, more singular in its identity. This is a reading of *agora* and *polis* that counters that offered within 'Plato's Pharmacy'. Indeed, despite 'Plato's Pharmacy' being understood to offer an exemplary critique of contemporary practice, its engagement with the *agora* is not mentioned within 'The Lecherous Professor Revisited'. Significantly, the *agora* is constituted by Derrida through an appeal to *différance* rather than as a site of self-sufficiency. Thus, in following Plato's precise formulations, Derrida understands the public space of '*polis* and *agora*' in terms of democracy, only to then construct this as the wandering, fatherless state of writing: 'At the disposal of each and of all, available on the sidewalks, isn't writing thus essentially democratic?' and isn't 'Democracy... orgy, debauchery, flea market, fair, a bazaar of constitutions where one can choose the one to make one's own'? (Derrida 2012 [1972], p. 145). Rather than turning upon object certainty here, the narrative of choice collapses the difference between seemingly determined objects, with the festive mood signalling not a liberating openness, but a *pharmakon* that can never be brought to light in a single moment: not son, democracy, agora and writing as separate entities that may be implicated in each other in a given discourse, but each constituted through the other prior to any being fixed as such. The objecthood that is necessary to the clear, public project, as it is framed within 'The Lecherous Professor Revisited', is other than itself; impossible to achieve on its own terms. It is a difficulty Derrida addresses when stating that:

> It is part of the rules of this game that the game should *seem to stop*. Then the *pharmakon*, which is older than either of the opposites, is 'caught' by philosophy, by 'Platonism' which is constituted by this apprehension, as a mixture of two pure, heterogeneous terms. (Derrida 2012 [1972], pp. 130–131)

The demand is always to secure, for example, 'the *agora*' *as is*, yet this will always meet with disappointment:

> The purity of the inside can then only be restored if the *charges are brought home against* exteriority as a supplement, inessential yet harmful to the essence, a surplus that *ought* never to have come to be added to the

untouched plenitude of the inside. The restoration of internal purity must then reconstitute, *recite*...that to which the *pharmakon* should not have had to be added. (Derrida 2012 [1972], p. 132)

This sacrificial structure, as it turns out, is not one that could be safely abstracted either from the *pharmakon* or the public space of the *agora*, in so far as Derrida reads it to be repeated in the rituals that kept Athens clean from external taint:

The character of the *pharmakos* has been compared to a scapegoat. The *evil* and the *outside*, the expulsion of evil, its exclusion out of the body (and out) of the city – these are the two major senses of the character and the ritual. (Derrida 2012 [1972], p. 131)

After a brief account of this ritual, which involves two of the 'most unsightly' people led outside the city to be beaten and perhaps burnt, Derrida states:

The city's body *proper* thus reconstitutes its unity, closes around the security of its inner courts, gives back to itself the word that links it with itself within the confines of the agora, by violently excluding from its territory the representative of an external threat or aggression. That representative represents the otherness of the evil that comes to affect the inside by unpredictably breaking into it. Yet the representative of the outside is nonetheless *constituted*, regularly granted its place by the community, chosen, kept, fed, etc, in the very heart of the inside... The ceremony of the *pharmakos* is thus played out on the boundary line between inside and outside, which it has as its function ceaselessly to trace and retrace. (Derrida 2012 [1972], p. 134)

Recitation, tracing and retracing; if the aim is to put the brakes on the game, to isolate one part from exterior influence, it will be found that the other returns, even in the movement of sacrifice. The fantasy of a world liberated from supplement cannot be sustained, and this is what I read to be played out in the scene of the *agora* in 'The Lecherous Professor Revisited'. The realm of the self-sufficient S-bend is premised on an openness that cannot tolerate *reading*, and the excess is formally banished, and purity seemingly restored. All is open to eye and hand. The *agora* is only thus made good, however, by a move that elsewhere brings home division and absence. I am referring here to the act of exclusion itself, of course, but also, for example: the return of the excluded other, and the damage that does to the security of the object; the repetitious structure that this requires, one never, by its nature, complete; the very notion of analogy and repetition, including that which I understand to return to my own reading, with its construction of 'Plato's Pharmacy' as a ghost text, a substitution, a supplement, one that frames as partial the scene of the *agora* as it is offered within 'The Lecherous Professor Revisited'. Counter to all this, there is no comfort to be had in a narrative of final collapse, in which difference is abolished, and openness, say, turns out to be closure and nothing more. The irresolvable nature of the *pharmakon* requires tension. The challenge is in understanding the impossibility of tracing this back to two or more contributing factors, available in their 'original', pure condition.[20]

As my reading of 'The Lecherous Professor Revisited' suggests, to close off the dangerous possibilities of one side is also to rehearse or stage the collapse of division, and it is in this that I take Derrida's reading of sacrifice to be instructive for contemporary debates concerning openness in Higher Education.[21] If one is ever tempted to neatly come down for once on one side of the divide outlined by Martin Paul Eve earlier, to constitute the university as an island removed from societal structures, or to promote an access that permits no division, there is always a risk of infection. When engaged in what I take to be the necessary task of asking questions of and about the university, and in critiquing the notion that the exclusive and elusive are privileged aspects of its functioning, we should be wary of promoting, instead, the seemingly unproblematic virtues of objecthood. If one can have sympathy with Diane Purkiss in her wish for an escape from occult, patriarchal provision, and thus turning, with positive relief, to figurations of smooth, delimited materiality, one should never forget that the certainty of the object, unproblematically available to vision, is crucial to 'The University of Excellence', and all the repressions and evasions it requires. Reading should not be sacrificed for the good of openness. What is openness without reading, after all? Not that reading is a prescription for resolving the tension between the open and the closed, nor does it offer liberation from technology.[22] Reading does not end anything, and even the notion that a detailed textual engagement would allow matters to be seen in all their complexity would require one already to have taken up a position on one side of the debate. Instead, I am taking reading to be difficult to place within a static model of knowledge. It is this understanding that drives the close reading that characterise this present book. I take textual, discursive engagement to be ongoing, dynamic and irreducible. In a culture of educational audit, this should not be too lightly dismissed.

Notes

1. Another problem with the defence of Faculty expertise, as suggested by arguments put forward by Bill Readings, is its dependence on notions of clear demarcations of identity, including self, subject and nation state that have been understood to have lost their purchase within contemporary life. See Readings (1996), pp. 44–53. It is here, I would argue, that Readings differs from Thomas Docherty. See Docherty, Thomas. 2015. *Universities at war*. London: Sage Swifts.
2. I had the privilege of being taught by Diane Purkiss at UEA in the early 90s. Purkiss was an inspirational teacher, and her writing continues to have a profound influence upon my thinking. She was also instrumental in my being accepted onto a postgraduate degree. Without Purkiss's influence, I would not be in my present academic post and would not be writing this.
3. For the former, see Deem, Rosemary, Hillyard, Sam and Reed, Michael. 2007. *Knowledge, higher education, and the new managerialism: The changing management of UK universities*. Oxford: Oxford University Press; Newman, Janet. 2001. *Modernising governance: New Labour, policy and society*. London: Sage. For the latter see Dennis, Dion. 1995. Brave new reductionism: TQM as ethnocentrism. *Education Policy Analysis Archives*, 3/9. http://epaa.asu.edu/ojs/article/view/652. Accessed 10 November 2016; Avis, James. 1996. 'The enemy within: Quality and managerialism in education'. In *Knowledge and nationhood: Education, politics and work*, eds. James Avis, Martin Bloomer, Geoff Esland, Denis Gleeson, and Phil Hodkinson, 105–120. London: Cassell/Continuum; Levidow, Les. 2006. Marketizing higher education. In *Neo-liberalism and educational reform*, eds. E. Wayne Ross and Rich Gibson, 237–256. New Jersey: Hampton; Docherty (2015).
4. This is quoted by Stefan Collini in his exacting critique of the appeal to Newman in contemporary accounts of Higher Education. See Collini, Stefan. 2012. *What are universities for?* London: Penguin, p. 45.
5. Michael Barber, quoted in Mead, Sara. 2006. Education reform lessons from England: An interview With Michael Barber. http://www.educationsector.org/analysis/analysis_show.htm?doc_id. Accessed 1 July 2016. See also Barber, Michael. 1996. *The Learning Game*. London: Indigo.
6. Deem et al. (2007), p. 10; Deem, Rosemary and Brehony, Kevin. 2005. Management as ideology. *Oxford Review of Education* 31/2: 217–235.
7. Lynch, Kathleen, Grummell, Bernie and Devine, Dympna. 2008. *New managerialism in education: Commercialization, carelessness and gender*. Basingstoke: Palgrave Macmillan; Webber, Michelle. 2008. Miss Congeniality meets the new managerialism: Feminism, contingent labour, and the new university. *Canadian Journal of Higher Education* 38/3: 37–56; Davies, Annette and Thomas,

Robyn. 2006. Managerialism and accountability in higher education: The gendered nature of restructuring and the costs to academic service. *Critical Perspectives on Accounting* 13/2: 179–193. Here I would especially recommend Parker, Ian. 2015. The function and field of speech and language in neoliberal society. *Organization* 17/3: 1–17: 'A reflexive attention to the role of "emotions" at work becomes part of the ethics of gendered care that ensures that occupants of positions of executive and middle management know their place, perform it, feel it' (7).

8. For 'clandestine', see Docherty (2015) above.
9. See Wright, Billie, Dziech, B. W. and Weiner, Linda. 1990. *The lecherous professor: Sexual harassment on campus.* Urbana: University of Illinois.
10. The extent to which such making visible will not necessarily lead to a more open and democratic scene of teaching can be gauged from the controversies surrounding the introduction of the Teaching Excellence Framework in the UK. See Patterson, Jess. 2015. TEF will mean more exploitation of academics on short term contracts. *Times Higher Education,* September 28.
11. It is worth stressing again the complexity, subtlety and self-reflexivity of Purkiss's work, qualities that I understand to set it apart from other texts discussed in this present book.
12. 'Space' itself is a problematic term in relation to 'Plato's Pharmacy', and to its account of patriarchal formulations. See the reading of the khora in Derrida (2012), p. 159, for example.
13. Purkiss (1994), p. 211. For more on care and carelessness in this context, see Lynch et al. (2012).
14. See Webber (2008).
15. Interestingly, for Purkiss, existing patriarchal provision results in precisely these limits, Purkiss (1994), p. 194. Although not discussed by Davies, I would also cite, for example, the high proportion of female post-graduate hourly-paid teachers within literature departments as another way in which the institutional structure is not favourable. For more, see Webber (2008).
16. See also, for example, Chris Lorenz's critique of the view that 'represents education as free and equal exchange between equally positioned buyers and sellers', in which 'the hierarchical relationship between teachers and those being taught disappears, and this suggests that the purchasers of education have a right to get what they have paid for'. Lorenz, Chris. 2012. If you're so smart, why are you under surveillance? Universities, neoliberalism, and New Public Management. *Critical Inquiry* 38: 599–629, 621.
17. The ironic return of a narrative of self-replication is inevitable, I would contend. My work, and the tensions within it, is not safely separable from 'The Lecherous Professor Revisited', for example. It is not comfortably outside the disruption of language to which it appeals. I will not try here to point out and second guess all of the ways in which my own reading is

17. caught up in an ironic return: for the difficulty of such a move see Lesnik-Oberstein, Karin. 2010. Childhood, queer theory and feminism. *Feminist Theory* 11/3: 309–321. It is for this reason that I am suspicious of arguments that insist upon the 'modest' nature of their enterprise. Such modesty demands that a text has an accurate assessment of its extent.
18. See also Ai Media. 'Making learning visible: First technology in education evaluation published. http://www.nesta.org.uk/blog/making-learning-visible-first-technology-education-evaluation-published. Accessed 1 June 2016.
19. For the idea of clarity within TED Talks, see the following: 'Clarity: Chris Anderson, the curator for TED Talks, explained this best in an interview: "*One of the most common killers is a lack of clarity. A presenter has a lot to say but they fail to put it together in a compelling and understandable narrative. There's too much jargon, or a bit too much chopping and changing. Some people will try to cram too much in, and the audience doesn't feel like it's been brought along on a thrilling journey*". Have an idea worth sharing. http://tedxfiu.com/have-an-idea-worth-sharing-be-a-tedxfiu-speaker/546. Accessed 1 June 2016. For an idea of the typically techno-utopian solutions to problems of university education offered by Ted Talks, see Shai Reshef. 2014. An ultra-low cost college degree. http://www.ted.com/talks/shai_reshef_a_tuition_free_college_degree. Accessed 1 June 2016. This is an argument for a tutor-free, online, and thus freely accessible university degree. There can be no lecherous professor here. Neither, however, can there be anything that is not instrumental. Education is understood in terms of eventual employment, the formative assessment is based on quizzes, the student does not have to meet anyone else during their learning, and the only options available are computer science or business administration. For more on neo-liberal and new managerial discourses of new technology, see Docherty (2015), pp. 64–69. For more on digitization and universalization in education see, Levidow (2006).
20. I read this move in the opening argument of 'The Lecherous Professor Revisited', but only in terms of the status of harassment. There it is claimed that 'the very notion that lechery can be expelled to purify the academy implies that lechery is a construction of the academy; the idea that the harasser's lechery is separable from his professorship locates it within his professorship.' Purkiss (1994), p. 191.
21. But what would constitute 'my reading'. How would it be possible to still the game and neatly separate 'my' language from that of 'The Lecherous Professor Revisited', for example? For more on the difficulties of a pure division within critiques of neo-liberal Higher Education discourse, see Parker (2015), especially pp. 9–11.
22. For the impossibility of liberating discourse from technology, see Wortham, Simon Moran. 2006. *Counter institutions: Jacques Derrida and the question of the university*. New York: Fordham University Press, pp. 101–103.

REFERENCES

AI Media. 2014. Abstract of NADP conference: Working for disability in higher education: The global perspective. http://nadp-uk.org/news/306/19/NADP-International-Conference-2015/d,News/. Accessed 1 June 2016.

Davies, Bronwyn. 2003. Death to critique and dissent? The policies and practices of new managerialism and of 'evidence-based practice'. *Gender and Education* 15/1: 91–103.

De Man, Paul. 1982. The resistance to theory. *Yale French Studies* 63: 3–20.

Derrida, Jacques. 2012 [1972]. Plato's pharmacy. In *Dissemination*, Trans. B Johnson, 67–186. London: Bloomsbury.

Docherty, Thomas. 2015. *Universities at war*. London: Sage Swifts.

Eve, Martin Paul. 2014. *Open access and the humanities*. Cambridge: Cambridge University Press.

House, Richard. 2014. Reimagining the university – an urgent cultural and paradigmatic imperative. http://www.criticalinstitute.org/re-imagining-university/. Accessed 1 July 2016

Lorenz, Chris. 2012. If you're so smart, why are you under surveillance? Universities, neoliberalism, and new public management. *Critical Inquiry* 38: 599–629.

Noble, David. 2001. *Digital diploma mills*. New York: Monthly Review Press.

Purkiss, Diane. 1994. The lecherous professor revisited: Plato, pedagogy and the scene of harassment. In *Rethinking sexual harassment*, eds. Clare Brant and Yun Lee Too, 187–219. London: Sage.

Readings, Bill. 1996. *The university in ruins*. Cambridge, MA, and London: Harvard University Press.

Visible Classroom. 2015. About - Visible Classroom. http://visibleclassroom.com/about/. Accessed 5 November 2016.

CHAPTER 3

Therapy and its Discontents: Bullying, Freedom and Self-Evidence in *The Dangerous Rise of Therapeutic Education* by Kathryn Ecclestone and Dennis Hayes

Abstract This chapter analyses *The Dangerous Rise of Therapeutic Education* by Kathryn Ecclestone and Dennis Hayes, and its 'radical humanist' claim that the focus upon subjective experience within contemporary 'therapeutic' pedagogy produces a 'diminished' learner. Ecclestone and Hayes understand bullying to be an 'infantilising' concept, encouraging unhelpful emotional introspection. Pulling oneself together in the pursuit of objective truth is therefore fundamentally *healthy*, an understanding that aligns *The Dangerous Rise* with the 'therapeutic turn' it questions. This chapter also reads the construction of bullying offered to be impossibly contradictory, and therefore something other than the stable, real-world category it is required to be. In conclusion, the difficulties in this account of bullying are read to be repeated in wider 'radical humanist' discussions of academic freedom within HE.

Keywords Radical humanism · Restorationist · Therapeutic education

1 Introduction

Anyone who has completed a Postgraduate Certificate in Academic Practice or Postgraduate Certificate in Education in the United Kingdom during the last twenty years will need little introduction to student-centred learning and the central position it occupies in contemporary provision. Distrust of a 'didactic' approach to education has resulted in a privileging of pedagogical strategies that claim to put the needs of the student first. Criticism of the discourse is often marginalised within teaching practice and in academic discussion to the point that it can seem that there is no viable alternative. Shortly before the Tory ascendancy, and Michael Gove's restorationist policies, however, a contrary discourse emerged, one that has gained a footing in Higher as well as Further, Secondary and Primary Education. This sets out to challenge what is taken to be a widespread institutional acceptance of learner-focused provision. Falling within the 'libertarian' school of 'radical humanism' pioneered by Frank Furedi, it claims that to grant students an active learning role does not lead to empowerment, as one can only make an active contribution to the world if granted access to authentic, independent knowledge.[1]

This chapter will offer a detailed analysis of the text that understands itself to be the first, sustained 'radical humanist' account of contemporary pedagogical issues, *The Dangerous Rise of Therapeutic Education* by Kathryn Ecclestone and Dennis Hayes (Ecclestone and Hayes 2009, pp. xii–xv). I will suggest that within this text the necessarily self-evident and stable real-world categories that are set against the discourse of student-centred learning ironically act as shifting, contradictory constructions. Although ostensibly opposed to the work of Diane Purkiss in its simple dismissal of the postmodern, and its scepticism towards identity politics and pedagogical innovation, I do read a shared resistance to reading, and an investment in self-evident materiality, one that, I would suggest, the text's own argument cannot sustain. The appeal to objective knowledge within *The Dangerous Rise of Therapeutic Education*, moreover, is understood to be indebted to the very subjectivity it attempts to master. I will conclude by suggesting that the difficulty 'radical humanism' has with separating itself wholly from the object of its criticism can be read in its celebration of 'freedom' within education. Turning to issues taken to be specific to Higher Education, I focus on both Academics For Academic Freedom, a group led by Dennis Hayes that claims to act against censorship, and a widely publicised article on emotion and political correctness on campus by Brendan O'Neill, editor of the Furedi-inspired online journal *Spiked!*

2 THE THERAPEUTIC TURN

As its title suggests, *The Dangerous Rise of Therapeutic Education* by Kathryn Ecclestone and Dennis Hayes argues against what it terms 'therapeutic education', initially defined as 'any activity that focuses on perceived emotional problems and which aims to make educational content and learning processes more "emotionally engaging"' (Ecclestone and Hayes 2009, p. x). On these terms, *The Dangerous Rise* reads itself as a critique of a broad contemporary consensus that validates pedagogy focused on the individual 'needs' of learners.[2] It is claimed that a concern with personal response leads to an interest in the process of education over its object, resulting in programmes that are inward looking and contentless (Ecclestone and Hayes 2009, p. 154).[3] This apparent transformation in provision is summed up for the text in a quotation from Mark Taylor, a history teacher working in South London: 'You know something has changed when young people want to know more about themselves than about the world' (Ecclestone and Hayes 2009, p. viii).

The Dangerous Rise argues that this alteration in education has been aided by an array of practices, from Circle Time in infant schools, where public confession of emotional vulnerability is understood to be mandatory, to Peer Mentoring and Learning to Learn in secondary schools, which are claimed to codify and regulate thought and action, all the way to the exit interviews and anti-bullying schemes that are read as forming an integral part of the structure of the emotionally invasive modern workplace, exemplified by the modern university. Such activities work together to offer a 'cultural script' that is internalised by the subjects exposed to it. 'Underlying' this 'script' is a 'therapeutic ethos', one that promotes the idea that all individuals are emotionally weak and should accept this weakness as part of their fundamental identity (Ecclestone and Hayes 2009, p. 128). It follows that education is no longer understood as having the power to transform the individual in any meaningful sense. In the past, so it is argued, education exposed its recipients to the best that had been thought and said. Acquiring this knowledge challenged preconceptions, enabling a transformation in attitudes. The active participant in student-led education is, in fact, a 'diminished' learner, one who should accept, even dwell, on their failings, unable to move beyond the condition into which they are initially socialised (Ecclestone and Hayes 2009, pp. 141–142). It is further claimed that such a construction contributes to a diminished idea of what it means to be human, reflecting and contributing to a profound disillusionment with the idea of progress, and the human ability to positively intervene in the world while justifying unprecedented institutional intrusion. The vulnerable subject is read as calling out for emotional support that government and employers are only too happy to supply.

The 'controversy' that *The Dangerous Rise* expects in response to its thesis arises in part from the text's willingness to reconcile a set of oppositions more usually understood to be absolute within educational theory.[4] For example, the discourse of 'student-centred learning' often sets itself in direct conflict with managerial approaches, the former's commitment to the emotional, the innovative, and the anti-authoritarian apparently working against the latter's investment in the quantitative and the centralising.[5] In this sense, the text's importance is understood to be bound up with its suggestion that the strategies to which the most seemingly radical of educationalists lend their support, contribute to, rather than challenge the spread of the 'authoritarian' (Ecclestone and Hayes 2009, p. 150). As *The Dangerous Rise* argues, 'Therapeutic Education' gains a vast level:

> of support for emotional interventions amongst policy makers and educators from liberal and Left traditions. In particular, our ideas challenge mantras of 'inclusive education', 'personalised learning' and 'learner voice', all embodied in the drive for a more personally relevant, engaging curriculum. (Ecclestone and Hayes 2009, p. xiv)

Although this is a thesis that is not articulated as often as the 'student-centredness' it questions, it is, I would contend, not as 'novel' as is suggested. It could be argued that comparably 'original and provocative critique[s]' of 'radical' theories of childhood are forwarded, for example, in the work of Erica Burman, Richard House, Karin Lesnik-Oberstein, Jan de Vos, and Valerie Walkerdine, theorists to whom this present book is indebted, not least because of their extended discussions of links between 'student-centred' education, liberalism, governmental intervention, psychologisation, globalisation, and the discourse of new managerialism.[6]

The failure to engage with this scholarship leads to a suggestion that a 'comprehensive' critique of the appeal to the emotional within education theory emerges in 2004 with Frank Furedi's *Therapy Culture* (Ecclestone and Hayes 2009, pp. 130–131). One possible reason for this neglect is that the theorists introduced earlier work within what could roughly be termed a tradition of 'construction'. They are interested in, for example, the kind of student that is necessitated by the various debates about provision, not with questions dependent on appeals to the non-discursive 'real'. For *The Dangerous Rise*, such moves are unhelpful, in the first instance, as they repeat that which they attempt to question, understood as they are to rely on what is termed the 'therapeutic fallacy', the idea that problems with therapy can be worked through without the need to wholly jettison questions pertaining to the subject, or work beyond a specific reading of Enlightenment rationalism. (Ecclestone and Hayes 2009, p. 152). For Ecclestone and Hayes, 'a therapeutic view of the pedagogical encounter... is prevalent in work critical of the logocentricism of enlightenment thought':

> Attacks on science and knowledge have parallels in the attack on the *knowing subject*. For example, post-modernists and others talk not about knowledge but 'knowledges' or mere stories or narratives and subjective accounts in the form of 'discourses'. In this parallel discussion, the self becomes our 'multiple selves', or identity becomes 'multiple identities' or, worse, 'fractured' or 'fragmented' identities. Understanding one's identity, multiple or fragmented identities and learning to live with them induce anxiety and endless introspective 'deconstruction': this encourages a therapeutic approach to education. (Ecclestone and Hayes 2009, pp. 152, 140)

It follows that Erica Burman or Richard House can apparently never move beyond the therapy they question, as they engage the indeterminate and readable, 'bring[ing] in uncertainty and doubt' rather than simply recognising the singular truth of the real (Ecclestone and Hayes 2009, p. 104).[7]

Although the aforementioned quotation is indicative of many of the problems I read in the critique of 'student-centred' or 'active' learning set out within *The Dangerous Rise*, I will limit myself at this early stage to a single issue, that of how 'understanding one's identity, multiple or fragmented identities and learning to live with them' is understood to 'induce anxiety and endless introspective "deconstruction"'. If the assertion is that 'post-modernist' discourse insists upon an anxious response to 'our multiple identities', one solution is simply to understand 'our multiple selves' with less anxiety. The text's insistence upon the collective ownership of these identities ensures, however, that any engagement with them is taken to be less than detached, while the 'parallel' nature of the discussion suggests that the 'multiple' is not a quality of the self as a 'genuine' object of knowledge, but a repetition of the pluralisation that is the hallmark of the 'post-modernist'. Moreover, as these 'multiple selves' are only ever available as 'mere stories', and because it is claimed that knowledge in the singular can only legitimately have a singular object (the self), the multiple can never be classed as an object of knowledge. Through legitimising 'discourse', however, if only as a dumping ground for all that is not singularly true, the text asks us, even if temporarily, to participate in an engagement with meaning independent of the concept and the object. Ironically, one result of this is to grant 'multiple identities' a strange singularity of signification. They are a 'story' that necessarily induces 'anxiety' in any party that seeks to 'understand' it. For a discourse devoid of true content, 'our "multiple identities"' is oddly resistant to being co-opted. If the possibility of an utterly independent 'discourse' suggests that truth is not required for signification, then the hard-impacted nature of that signification allows it a rigidity, a resistance to response, that might be taken to be truth itself. This resistance also constructs the individual attempting to understand 'discourse' in an oddly 'therapeutic' fashion, with the 'diminished' human subject powerless to respond to the 'multiple identities' in any other than the anxious way 'induced' by it.

Against this construction of 'discourse' is placed one of objective truth. The only way in which the therapeutic can be resisted is apparently through a process of 'initiation' into distinct 'forms' of knowledge, including mathematics, physical sciences, moral knowledge, philosophy, history, literature and art. It is claimed that 'to enter this common inheritance of human achievement through education is "the only way of becoming a human being, and to inhabit it is to be a human being..." Not to inhabit it is to be less than human' (Ecclestone and Hayes 2009, p. 142, quoting Michael Oakeshott). An appeal to the physicality of this knowledge can be read. It is an inheritance, something stable enough to be passed down. It exists before one encounters it. One enters it, it having physical dimensions, and then one dwells within it as an environment. One never alters it, apart, perhaps, to add to it. Despite being understood as fundamentally external to the self, it is constitutive of one's identity as a human. The text suggests that part of the reason why a commitment to such subject knowledge has been lost is that 'many educationalists and teachers see children as incapable of education because they are no longer seen as truly human' (Ecclestone and Hayes 2009, p. 143). Yet there is a sense in which, according to this argument, no child is human. Humanity is something they have the potential to achieve: every child is an 'heir to an inheritance' of humanity only. 'Humanity', in this construction, is something prior to the child, while also located in its future. The child's 'humanity' exists before them as something that is not them, a complete identity that is oddly lacking, waiting, as it is, to be dwelt within.

There are, then, two distinct phases of life, two modes of being: the human and the pre-human. The problem with the current provision is apparently that the child exists in a pre-human state, this pedagogy failing to move it 'beyond narrow personal and social concerns and problems' (Ecclestone and Hayes 2009, p. 143). 'Therapeutic education' focuses on the 'emotional' side of the subject, and on the 'self', an aspect of the subject that is subjective and 'interested'. The part of the subject capable of dwelling within its 'inheritance', the part that is necessarily 'disinterested' is the 'intellectual or cognitive (which we would argue is the essence of the person)' (Ecclestone and Hayes 2009, p. 152).

Previously, 'our "multiple selves"' was read as so far from any notion of independent truth that it could not be granted the status of concept, existing at the level of discourse only, a sleight of language not corresponding to anything beyond a closed-off system of signification. Yet the condition of being 'human' is one that requires a subject divided between 'human' and 'pre-human' existence, between subjective and objective states, between 'essence' and supplement. In my reading, the problem of a split or fractured identity to which *The Dangerous Rise* finds itself committed results from its own insistence upon division. It is the desire for a truth untarnished by language, an objectivity never implicated in subjective judgment, which makes the appeals to the wholeness of truth, to the radical inclusivity of presence, difficult to sustain.[8] We are back to the problem of the scapegoat, as discussed in the previous chapter, and the division that can never achieve the purity it moves to ensure.

3 Bullying

For *The Dangerous Rise*, the problems introduced through a rejection of the singular and certain in favour of a pedagogy centred on, and authored by, students can be seen especially in the rise of the discourse of bullying, one that is claimed to be increasingly employed in 'adult' situations, with Ecclestone and Hayes focusing on the experiences of those working within Higher and Further Education. This is read as indicative of a wider culture that cannot access structures previously employed to negotiate conflict at work. Instead of, for example, trade unions working with management to resolve issues of exploitation, there are therapists helping individual victims seek recognition from individual 'bullies'. It is claimed that:

> Fighting against the bullies has become the new form of struggle in the workplace. It has the benefit of being a simple, mono-conceptual view of the world without any of the conceptual and linguistic demands of 'exploitative', 'oppressive' or 'authoritarian'. It is the cry from the playground. (Ecclestone and Hayes 2009, p. 112)

As for *The Dangerous Rise*, 'fighting against the bullies' is a 'cry' projected from 'the playground', it is one that comes from a place, rather than the lips of an individual subject. It is a collective cry, or an inhuman 'cry'. This 'cry' could simply be positioned against 'human' utterance, the sound of the environment, the socialising aspect devoid of any sense of active, 'correctly' socialised subjecthood. If on the other hand, the 'cry' is read as human articulation, this is a human that enjoys less individuality, even less humanity, than that which should be found in the workplace, one reduced to the exteriority of its conditioning. This is in keeping with the construction of the child as 'pre-human' analysed previously: 'the playground' is a place of childhood within this formulation, and childhood is signified by its failure to offer individually authored, rational language.

There is, however, a contrary sense in which the 'cry' may also be read as the voice of the adult in 'the workplace' masquerading as, or adopting the persona of, the child in 'the playground'. Thus there is a conflicting account of origins and their worth at play. Although the 'cry' can be read as sourced in a realm of childhood – the original condition of childhood being marked by a lack of awareness as to what constitutes appropriate speech, a failure to understand the context in which its language will finally be received, an inability to read the future – it may also be traced back to an adult realm, with the adult marked by its refusal to engage with the genuine condition of 'the workplace' – a failure to understand the inappropriateness of the childish 'cry' for the environment it finds itself in, an inability to recognise the present.

It is also possible to read the cry of 'bully' not only as a child's failure to comprehend the reality of the adult workplace, or an adult inability to do the same, but as the product of a child's misrecognition of its immediate, playground situation. In this formulation, the difference between adult and child is that the former should see the 'real world' forces that lead to certain behavioural patterns, whereas the latter somehow intrinsically cannot see them, or tend not to or do not need to. Such a move allows adult and child to inhabit the same existence, one that is somehow objectively knowable from an informed, adult point of view, with the social forces that shape 'the workplace' not shut out by the school gates, yet with childhood read as a state in which misrecognition of such forces is expected.

Such a construction of 'the playground' as that which adults, at least, should understand to be a social and political environment is, however, questioned at certain stages of the argument set out within *The Dangerous Rise*. Rather than the child being ignorant of vast social forces, the text suggests that the discourse of 'bullying' lends the seriousness of definition to that which is more often than not merely 'playground rough and tumble'. Anything that is a little physical, boisterous or 'forceful or demanding' is apparently misrecognised as 'bullying' (Ecclestone and Hayes 2009, p. 112). So within 'the playground' there is a failure to recognise what is 'really' going on in 'the playground', cut off from wider reality as it apparently is through what is taken to be its game playing actuality and the misrecognition that is claimed to characterise childhood perception. What is 'really' going on is nothing of importance: the hidden realm is not one of vast, signifying structures, but of individual acts of boisterousness. Indeed, the very insistence on the 'cry' emanating from 'the playground' rather than, say, 'the classroom', allows the 'truth' of bullying to be constructed in terms of its triviality, its playfulness, its separation from the adult.

If the voice of 'the playground' is understood to be one that fails to recognise the 'truth' of bullying's non-existence, then slogans to be read within 'the workplace' – specifically the university workplace – fail to remember its actuality:

> Don't bully me! I'm a lecturer!
>
> The slogan above was a suggestion to produce stickers for lecturers in a new university to wear. The lessons of the playground had clearly not been learnt in that institution or it would be common knowledge that such things would get you tied to the whiteboard! (Ecclestone and Hayes 2009, p. 112)

Thus, according to *The Dangerous Rise*, lecturers do not remember or are alienated from the 'reality' of bullying. Bullying *does* exist at this stage of the argument; it is a physical enterprise, with its own logic. It is also read as educational, in that it gives lessons, an interesting construction given the text's broader understanding of successful education as a matter of 'submission' rather than active participation (Ecclestone and Hayes 2009, p. 101). Hayes and Ecclestone write here in what can be taken to be a 'humorous' fashion, the humour deriving from the failure to recognise the violent 'reality' of bullying, the workplace claims concerning bullying being trivial in comparison. Yet this violent 'reality' has itself been read as an irrelevance: childish, unconnected with wider social forces, 'rough and tumble' merely.

The Dangerous Rise ignores such contradictions and proceeds to compare the 'reality' of bullying (at this stage constructed as the act of tying up the 'me' that exclaims about bullying, or insists on not being bullied) to that which passes for bullying in the workplace:

> not being recognised or valued for teaching or research; having someone raise their voice, be rude, or even 'shout' at a colleague; feeling too intimidated to speak up in a staff meeting.... We've even heard of 'bullying' e-mails!...To top all this, we have heard the forceful expression of opinions, ideas and argument called 'soft bullying'. (Ecclestone and Hayes 2009, pp. 112–113)

The self-evidence of e-mail's intrinsic resistance to being co-opted as a tool for 'bullying' is apparently such that an exclamation mark can serve as justification. Yet if it is so clearly untrue, as the exclamation mark suggests, why is it necessary for the text to argue against it? In this, the text not only fails to sustain the idea that it is self-evident that bullying does not occur in university environments, the arguments it utilises contradicts previous statements about the reality of bullying amongst children. For example, it is claimed that through focusing on bullying in the workplace adults are being asked 'to tackle a problem that simply does not exist outside of the playground' (Ecclestone and Hayes 2009, p. 113). It would seem that this specific thing, 'bullying', finally does (again) exist in 'the playground', rather than being misrecognised 'boisterousness'. It is, however, unclear what such 'bullying' might be, whether an objective 'fact' of playground existence, or a misrecognition on the part of school children, the actions of a minority that should be condemned, or a general occurrence it would be foolish not to condone.

It is the first of these options to which Dennis Hayes appeals when, in an earlier article concerned with issues in Further Education entitled 'Being bullied? Just grow up!', he claims that '"bullying" is a concept that has been imported from the playground into the workplace' (Hayes 2004). Here, the school is isolated from the rest of the social world: bullying has not emerged within 'the playground' due to any factors outside of it. It is an idea taken up by writers on bullying and education sympathetic to the arguments put forward by *The Dangerous Rise*. For example Helene Guldberg, author of *Reclaiming Childhood: Freedom and Play in an Age of Fear* and managing editor of *Spiked!*, claims that what is thought of as 'bullying' arises from 'the spontaneous dynamics of playground life' and, as such, adults should refrain from intervening (Guldberg 2008). The playground is understood as a place with its own self-contained laws, its own 'dynamics'. Because such arguments are rooted in a rejection of social intervention, a given social situation must be read as inevitable, the product of a childhood understood to be entirely enclosed and self-creating. It could be argued that with this idea of naturally unfolding development, and the requirement to refrain from intervention, *The Dangerous Rise* and its supporters move dangerously close to the position that they wish to attack, the 'therapeutic' discourse of child-centeredness, with 'bullying' constructed in terms of a pedagogy that must remain self-contained and student-authored.[9]

The Dangerous Rise is required to appeal to a 'natural' education resistant to intervention in order for it to read the states of childhood and adulthood, the human and the pre-human, as separate. This is despite such a move running counter to the restorationist dislike of an education in which students are 'presented as people who "are what they are", and who are therefore only motivated to learn what is immediately relevant to their own personal lives and interests' (Ecclestone and Hayes 2009, p. 143). The desire for such separation can be read throughout the text. In the quotation concerning the 'cry from the playground', this section began by analysing, for example, the inappropriateness of the 'cry' can be read as arising from the adult violating the space of 'the playground' as much as 'the playground' authoring what should be adult speech. Yet the separation is never quite as stable as it is required to be. What, after all, does it mean to say that the 'cry' of 'bully' 'turns us all into children'? Within the various arguments offered by *The Dangerous Rise*, this could suggest that we have become genuinely isolated from the reality of social forces, or simply made ignorant of them, or that our ignorance is responsible for their disappearance. For its argument to hold, and despite its appeal to the stability and self-evidence of categories, 'childhood' is understood to be impossibly divided.

4   'Just Being at Work'

One reason for such uncertainty has already been introduced, as despite the discourse of bullying being read as a misrecognition of the objective truth of social and economic conflict, it is also understood to be productive of a de-politicised reality. In other words, it is a discourse signified by a retreat from the world, yet one that has 'real world' effects. Despite it altering our worldview, however, leading to a postmodern society rooted in 'culture' rather than 'politics', the discourse of 'bullying' can be understood as something separate from the truth of what is (Ecclestone and Hayes 2009, p. 143). Take the following quotation from 'Being bullied? Just grow up!'

> So many other common experiences in FE can bring an accusation of bullying: having to re-apply for a post; suddenly being moved with all your books and papers to another office; being spoken to with a raised voice, or shouted at; even finding out that your colleagues don't respect or even like you, the tendency in all the cases is to answer with a categorical 'YES!' or a cautious 'it could be!'. But the grown–up answer is 'No it's not. It's just being at work.' (Hayes 2004)

Here 'bullying' can be separated from 'just being at work'. The discourse is simply misrecognition of what is, apparently, genuinely there. This means that shouting at people, for example, is understood as intrinsically distinct from a separate and secondary misrecognition, the discourse of bullying. In my reading, this naturalises 'shouting at people' within the workplace, resisting the sense in which it is part of a particular understanding of work, a discourse of appropriate action. Rather than self-evidently opposed to what *The Dangerous Rise* takes to be an infantilizing discourse, 'shouting at people' can be read as an 'emotional' and 'irrational' form of communication. Instead of a real world object of misrecognition, I take it to be a precise linguistic construct that constitutes a way of understanding and organising the world. It is productive of meaning, situating adult interaction in terms of the contentless and uni-directional, as well as the hierarchical and aggressive.

That 'shouting at people' is not read as narrational within *The Dangerous Rise* should not, perhaps, come as a surprise, as throughout the text there is a repeated refusal to engage with that which lacks the certainty of self-evidence, rather than any sustained attempt to question its existence. It is this refusal that, alongside a propensity to shout at people, is understood to characterise mature thought, at least in so far as it is indicative of a move beyond a child-authored education, one appealed to in the work of all 'radical humanists' of the *Spiked!* school. For example, Dennis Hayes expresses concern that:

> Proponents of playground concepts suggest that people should not be afraid to speak up and express feelings of vulnerability. This turns us all into children. Don't expose your vulnerabilities at work. Grow up, get a grip, and life in the Cinderella service might really start to improve. (Hayes 2004)[10]

'Gett[ing] a grip' is read in terms of a lack of speech: it is 'speaking up' as much as expressing 'feelings of vulnerability' that seems to be the problem. An opposition is constructed between the certainty of gripping, and the lack of security of vulnerable, exposed, verbal childhood. What is important is control, its lack signified by speech. To speak is to make oneself vulnerable because one's interior becomes available to another. This, apparently, is the condition of the child. The child can be understood, and this is its problem, a problem that arises from speech. Yet this childish speech also defies true understanding because it is 'subjective' and 'emotional' rather than rationalistic and it is claimed that 'emotions, after all, cannot be questioned. They just are' (Ecclestone and Hayes 2009, p. 98). It seems, then, that speech, as emotional, is meaningless, having no status beyond its mere existence. Being existent rather than meaningful does not, however, lead emotions to be understood as things in themselves, as is the case within the philosophy of Nigel Thrift to be read in the following chapter, but as that which is least real and most discursive. It seems that the excess of language allows the 'childish' individual to be the most and least obvious of subjects, that which makes itself vulnerable by communicating its 'inner' meaning in an uncontrolled fashion, and that which has no meaning to communicate, a thing of blank exteriority.

The child is not always understood in terms of an excess of language, however, as at other stages of the argument put forward by *The Dangerous Rise* it is signalled by linguistic absence. The cry from the playground is wordless, after all. In a move comparable to its insistence that the child is the most and least obvious of categories, the text suggests that the problem of language is that it is both excessive and lacking. If the excess of language signifies a lack of control, a pre-human failure to adequately grasp the meaning and a childish habit of self-exposure, then its absence produces utterance devoid of meaning, an emotional, inhuman, childish 'cry'.

It would seem that it is an easy thing to lose control, with too much or too little language leading the subject to the same state of inhumanity. It is imperative for this argument, then, that the child learns to control itself, as it is only with supreme self-control that one can effect real change in the world and gain certain knowledge of it. Yet this leads the proponents of 'radical humanism' to take what, for them, is a problematic position, one in which the pedagogical function is to offer advice on how to live. In arguing against the therapeutic, Hayes finds that he must offer the 'emotional' subject the correct psychological response to their situation: grow up, get a grip, do not expose yourself, this way lies happiness.

The Dangerous Rise, of course, claims to reject any form of education that focuses on theories of reception, only being interested in 'education for its own sake', this requiring the study of a body of knowledge that is independent of the individual student (Ecclestone and Hayes 2009, p. 141). Yet it can only do so by offering up its own, 'correct' reading of the psychology of response. *The Dangerous Rise* has no need for the disciplinary technologies utilised by therapy because it claims to know the important aspect of the student's mind. The other part, the emotional, does not escape knowledge either, at least at one stage of its argument, as the child and the childish adult who rely upon this aspect are constructed as constantly exposing themselves to scrutiny.

Despite working against the notion of a socialisation that coaches 'the appropriate dispositions and attitude of the emotionally well citizen', the argument against the 'therapeutic turn' cannot abandon psychological instruction. The demand for the subject to adopt a 'self-renunciatory character' does not avoid what is understood to be the 'internal' realm of psychology (Ecclestone and Hayes 2009, pp. 161, 124). Rather, the rejection of 'bullying' articulates the therapeutic power of renunciation.

A comparative move can be read when the text attempts to answer potential criticism of its lack of robust evidence. As introduced earlier, in attempting to clarify its reading of empiricism and rationality, *The Dangerous Rise* makes an appeal to what it terms 'logocentricism', a philosophy that is understood to claim that objects in the world are present 'things in themselves', requiring no interpretation.[11] Hayes and Ecclestone also require a notion of truth hidden beneath appearance, however, that which, after Furedi, they name the 'public's' relational 'system of meaning' (Ecclestone and Hayes 2009, p. x). Because, according to *The Dangerous Rise*, this contemporary public understanding is never explicitly announced, it being an 'unarticulated vision', it can only be accessed through 'examples' (Ecclestone and Hayes 2009, pp. xiii, 147). The tension between these two moves remains unresolved, the truth of the world being a matter of hard impacted objecthood, and a hidden ideology accessible only through the object as symptom. Remarkably, this lack of consistency in the construction of external truth results at one stage in it being replaced by an appeal to the audience: '[w]e do not claim to offer these arguments as systematic empirical evidence... We ask readers to decide if our examples and the conclusions we draw from them resonate with experiences in their own context' (Ecclestone and Hayes 2009, p. xiii). So 'the reader' exists within an individual 'context' rather than in a continuous reality, and this is defined in terms of 'experience' rather than intellect: it is this 'reader' who ultimately decides on the truth of the text's arguments, a judgement that is to be based on 'resonation', rather than any systematic comparison.

This is indicative of what I read to be the text's failure to extricate itself from the much derided move by which the value of education is understood in terms of its effects, with *The Dangerous Rise* suggesting that '[p]laying with children's feelings is personally damaging and profoundly un-educational and we have offered reasons for our view throughout the book' (Ecclestone and Hayes 2009, p. 147). Thus the restorationist agenda is fundamentally good for people, and it is good for people because *The Dangerous Rise* has an utterly secure grasp of psychological response, what is 'personally', subjectively damaging and what is not. In a similar vein, Helene Guldberg can claim that 'bullying' is not a problem because 'children are not emotionally scarred by these experiences' and that adult intervention helps only to 'undermine children's ability to manage uncomfortable situations' (Guldberg 2008). This is apparently simply the truth of the matter.

The Dangerous Rise claims to offer a way out of a de-politicised, 'postmodern' morass that is student-centred education, wherein arguments are dependent on theories of response, humans are robbed of their humanity, little respect is given to academic subjects, and objects in the real world can no longer be taken to be sufficient in themselves. In my reading, however, this leads to an argument based on a partial engagement with the enlightenment tradition, in which children are understood to be inhuman and isolated from political and social forces, theories of education are justified through appeals to their real world effects, and 'bullying' is taken to be: an aspect of reality; a misrecognition of that reality; an aspect of reality that is not really real; a rare, yet serious, aberration; a consistent, reactive, system of violence; so much trivial boisterousness.

5 'Radical Humanism' in Higher Education

This sense in which radical humanism partakes of that which it would condemn can be read in its recent contributions to debates concerning academic freedom within Higher Education. Take, for example, 'Free speech is so last century', a 2014 article on student activism for *The Spectator* by Brendan O'Neill, the editor of *Spiked! Online*, and contributor to the recent *Unsafe Space: The Crisis of Free Speech on Campus* (2016). In the article, O'Neill contends that an adherence to political correctness has resulted in universities treating their students like 'children', shielding them from offense, and thus the experience of meeting intellectually challenging ideas. For O'Neill: 'It's hard to think of any other section of society that has undergone as epic a transformation as students have. From freewheelin' to ban-happy, from askers of awkward questions to suppressors of offensive speech, in the space of a generation' (O'Neill 2014). After a brief overview of what students have found offensive, he concludes that '[s]afety from physical assault is one thing – but safety from words, ideas, Zionists, lads, pop music, Nietzsche? We seem to have nurtured a new generation that believes its self-esteem is more important than everyone else's liberty' (O'Neill 2014). One difficulty here is that, within an argument premised on separation – that of adult and child, for example – the separation of 'words, ideas' and physical assault is not always this clear cut. Take O'Neill's claim that students should enjoy being 'mind-battered by offensiveness'. Words and ideas are constructed as assault, and this is framed as a good thing. It is a line of reasoning that is not sustained, however, as the spur to writing the article was that O'Neill 'was attacked by a swarm of Stepford students this week' (O'Neill 2014). It might be supposed either that this was a physical assault, with words and ideas being irrelevant, or a verbal attack, and thus inevitably an enjoyable 'mind battering'. It transpires that neither is the case. The 'attack' involved a 'mob' of students setting up a Facebook page in which they 'robotically utter[ed] the same stuff about feeling offended' by the fact that a debate concerning abortion to which O'Neill was to contribute did not feature a female speaker. Further 'attacks' variously involve O'Neill being 'circled by Stepfords after taking part in a debate on faith schools', being 'harangue[d]', 'branded a "denier"', 'jeered at' and 'lambasted' (O'Neill 2014).[12] As none of this is understood to constitute a debate, O'Neill is not required to enjoy his discomfort. Students, however, are understood to encounter 'words and ideas' in a different fashion:

> Where once students might have allowed their eyes and ears to be bombarded by everything from risqué political propaganda to raunchy rock, now they insulate themselves from anything that might dent their self-esteem and, crime of crimes, make them feel 'uncomfortable'. (O'Neill 2014)

To be a passive subject 'bombarded' by 'raunchy rock' is one thing, according to this argument, to be 'harangued' by students quite another. In going some way to justify this discrepancy, O'Neill changes the precise terms of his objection to the 'Stepford Students', the problem with them no longer centring on their lambasting and jeering:

> In each case, it wasn't the fact the students disagreed with me that I found alarming – disagreement is great! – it was that they were so plainly shocked that I could have uttered such things, that I had failed to conform to what they assume to be right, that I had sought to contaminate their campuses and their fragile grey matter with offensive ideas. (O'Neill 2014)

What alarms is the shock expressed by another, their inability to comprehend. As it stands, however, the lack of understanding is all on one side. O'Neill knows only too well the thoughts of the students, the reason behind their shock, which is so 'plain...': 'I had sought to contaminate their campuses and their fragile grey matter with offensive ideas'. For all the plainness of the revelation, I am unclear what is being claimed at this stage. Is it that the students share O'Neill's understanding of their having 'fragile grey matter', for example? Is it precisely the threat to matter thus understood that shocks them? Or is what is 'plain' constituted from a narrative perspective on the students, the clarity of the situation requiring the student's thought to be framed by a perspective other than their own?

In my reading, the appeal to 'grey matter' is worth thinking about in a little more detail, as it can be read to be at odds with other claims within the article. Thus, for example, the students are also condemned by O'Neill because they are outraged 'that two human beings "who do not have uteruses" should get to hold forth on abortion – identity politics at its most basely biological' (O'Neill 2014). As biological reductivism is such a problem, why, it might be asked, is it acceptable to construct student thought and individuality in terms of 'fragile grey matter'? This appeal to the biological mind is repeated in the article's distrust of the idea that culture can have a direct influence on thinking, hence the questioning of the way in which 'the urge to re-educate apparently corrupted minds, have been swallowed whole by a new generation' who offer 'censorious, misanthropic arguments about culture determining behaviour' and 'warps minds' and 'that is why it is right for students to strive to keep such wicked, misogynistic stuff as the Sun newspaper and sexist pop music off campus' (O'Neill 2014). Once again, however, the argument offered by O'Neill is not immune to such criticism, with, for example, its contention that 'student brains have been replaced by brains bereft of critical faculties and programmed to conform', and that the 'Stepford students' have merely 'mechanical minds' (O'Neill 2014). The argument is that pornography, or 'male only' debates about the ethics of female reproduction, or Rugby club literature criticizing 'homosexual debauchery' clearly have no effect on thinking, while exposure to a politically correct environment will alter the very structure of the brain. Two questions, then: does environment have an effect on thinking or not? And is there a point at which it ceases to be enjoyable to be bombarded?

I will conclude this chapter by briefly drawing attention to Academics For Academic Freedom (AFAF), a pressure group set up and organised by Dennis Hayes, the signatories to which include a large number of individuals with links to *Spiked!* I make the connection, as it seems to me that the double standard outlined previously, also evidenced in the problematic totality of the separation between 'therapeutic' and 'radical humanist' education addressed at length in this chapter, finds repetition in its work. On its website, the AFAF states that it:

> was founded in 2006 as a campaigning group for all lecturers, academic-related staff, students and researchers who wanted to defend unimpeded enquiry and expression. It began with a statement of Academic Freedom which lecturers and others could sign but has since taken up the case for free speech and academic freedom around the world. AFAF is also heavily involved in case work much of which never hits the headlines. (AFAF 2015)

Hayes has claimed that AFAF 'supports any academic whose freedom is under attack, whether it agrees with what they say or not', a claim that stems from a conviction that 'if we start started saying "no" to anybody who wanted to stop any freedom of speech, then you take the first step towards actually rebuilding a rational society' (AFAF 2015). Despite this generosity, those cases that do hit the headlines are remarkably consistent, with AFAF lending its support to a string of academics accused of racism, including Frank Ellis, James Watson, David Coleman, and Nicholas Kollerstrom (Hayes 2010). Taking an article written by the first of these, a difficulty with Hayes's notion of academic freedom can be read:

> Higher education is now expected to be inclusive which means that it must host a miscellany of pseudo-intellectual misfits – gender studies and black studies are two obvious examples – which are hostile to notions of intellectual rigour, objective truth, evidence and, above all, as this author can personally attest, to free speech and academic freedom. Gender studies and black studies have no place in a university: they are little more than grievance factories; they should be targeted for immediate closure. Vice-chancellors, university secretaries, the heads of departments and schools, who do not defend the essentials of a university for reasons of ideological and financial expediency, or who fail out of plain cowardice to confront the charlatans, cease to preside over a university. (Ellis 2010)

What is the intention of 'targeting' 'Gender studies and black studies... for immediate closure' if not a closing down of debate? Crucially, Hayes shares with Ellis more than a distrust of discourses that are critical of 'objective truth', as discussed in the introduction to this present chapter: in *The Dangerous Rise* he argues that spreading the light of reason requires certain approaches and subjects to be outside the bounds of the university. Thus, for example, for Ecclestone and Hayes, university provision should not be concerned with 'uncertainty and doubt' and 'we argue that there is room for emotion in education only as the passionate pursuit of truth in the sciences and the study of beauty and human emotion in the arts' (Ecclestone and Hayes 2009, pp. 153–154). As such material is understood to be, unfortunately, part of university provision at present, Hayes and Ecclestone have a suggestion as to how it should be met: counter to O'Neill's distress at being 'harangued', *The Dangerous Rise* despairs of a situation in which 'at research conferences, poor or boring papers are listened to with respect' (Ecclestone and Hayes 2009, p. 98).[13] The suggestion is, then, that debate should occur in a disrespectful environment. An approach that manages to combine such disrespect with the avoidance addressed earlier can be read in a letter from Hayes to *The Times Education Supplement* concerning 'postmodernism':

> Talking to an eminent sociologist who had been accused of being perfunctory with postmodern thinkers, he gave me the answer that I think is one we should all take to heart before the misanthropic disease of postmodernity gets a stronger hold . . . : 'When you see shit in the road you step over it, not in it.' (Hayes 2008)[14]

Racism is never to be avoided, but postmodernity is a 'shit' with which one must not come into contact. And everything is up for debate, as long as the emotions, and 'doubt' and 'pessimism' about knowledge are not on the agenda. The AFAF declares that '[i]f academics can't debate, then academia is dead. If it is to be kept alive, academics have to defend the right to debate anything and everything' (AFAF 2015). I take it from this that tolerance is limited to the subjects debated, not the terms of the debate itself. Any theoretical approach that questions the frame is to be excluded.[15] In this way, *The Dangerous Rise* can keep itself insulated from the kind of critique I offer here, and my central contention that, as an ideology, 'radical humanism' is self-condemned.

NOTES

1. This is a way of thinking common to a group of UK intellectuals who left The Revolutionary Communist Party in the late 1990s to set up a variety of broadly libertarian organisations, including *Spiked!*, Sense About Science, and The Institute of Ideas. See *Spiked! Online*. 2016. http://www.spiked-online.com/. Accessed 18 January 2016; Sense About Science. 2016. http://www.senseaboutscience.org/. Accessed 18 January 2016; Institute of Ideas. 2016. http://www.instituteofideas.com/. Accessed 18 January 2016.
2. See also, for example, Williams, Joanna. 2016. *Academic freedom in an age of conformity: Confronting the fear of knowledge*. Basingstoke: Palgrave; Furedi, Frank. 2009. *Wasted: Why education isn't educating*. London: Continuum; Bristow, Jennie and Furedi, Frank. 2008. *Licensed to hug: How child protection policies are poisoning the relationship between the generations and damaging the voluntary sector*. London: Civitas; Guldberg, Helene. 2009. *Reclaiming childhood*. Abingdon: Routledge.
3. The text reads itself as opposing 'Conservative' agendas: 'Conservative interest in the vague aspects of the self is the opposite of radical humanistic education', p. 162. Yet the Conservative government in Britain has a long history of

promoting 'restorationist' policy. See, for example, Stephen J. Ball quoting Kenneth Clarke's claim that discourses of individualised learning 'overlook the way in which any human activity ... will contain a mass of customary and traditional knowledge and skills'. Ball, Stephen. 1994. *Education reform.* Buckingham: OUP, p. 42. For an extended critique of the kind of restorationist discourse of 'submission' advocated by Ecclestone and Hayes (Ecclestone and Hayes 2009, p. 101) from an alternative 'humanist' perspective, see Law, Stephen. 2006. *The war on children's minds.* Abingdon: Routledge.

4. See, for example, Beckmann, Andrea and Cooper, Charlie. 2004. 'Globalisation', the new managerialism and education: Rethinking the purpose of education in Britain. *Journal for Critical Education Policy Studies* 2/2. http://www.jceps.com/wp-content/uploads/PDFs/02-2-05.pdf. Accessed 6 November 2016. For an extended discussion, see Burman, Erica. 2008. *Deconstructing developmental psychology.* New York: Routledge; Cocks, Neil. 2009. *Student-centred: Education, freedom and the idea of audience.* Ashby-de-la-Zouch: Inkermen/Axis Series.

5. For a classic account, see Rogers, Carl. 1983. *Freedom to learn for the 80 s.* New York: Merrill.

6. See Erica Burman (2008); Walkerdine, Valerie, Henriques, Julian, Hollway, Wendy, Urwin, Cathy and Venn, Couze. 1984. *Changing the subject: Psychology, social regulation and Subjectivity.* London: Routledge; House, Richard and Loewenthal, Del. 2012. The rise of therapeutic education: Beneficent, uncertain, or dangerous? *Self and Society* 39/3: 6–18; De Vos, Jan. 2012. *Psychologisation in times of globalisation.* London: Routledge; Lesnik-Oberstein, Karin. 1994. *Children's literature: Criticism and the fictional child.* Oxford: Clarendon; Lesnik-Oberstein, Karin, Burman, Erica, Parker, Ian et al. 2015. Let UK universities do what they do best – teaching and research. *The Guardian*, July 6. See also, for example, Neubert, Stefan. 2010. Democracy and education in the twenty-first century: Deweyan pragmatism and the question of racism. *Education Theory* 60/4: 487–522; Anglin-Jaffe, Helen. Reading the 'happy child': Normative discourse in wellbeing education. In *Children in culture revisited*, ed. Karin Lesnik-Oberstein, 73–89. Basingstoke: Palgrave Macmillan.

7. Counter to this I would support Erica Burman's contention that '[e]xploitation and oppression suffuse the structure of developmental psychology. Our task is to deconstruct it', Burman, Erica. 2008. *Deconstructing developmental psychology*, 2nd edn. London: Routledge, p. 303. See also Richard House's argument that '[t]herapy, in its modern profession-centred form, increasingly functions as a "regime of truth" whose discourse actively creates identity and subjectivity... and whose accompanying practices self-fulfillingly construct and ideological framework which then reinforces and guarantees the conditions of its own existence', House, Richard. 2003. *Therapy*

beyond modernity: Deconstructing and transcending profession-centred therapy. London: Karnac, p. 14. For Ecclestone and Hayes, doubt is opposed to rationalism. A comparative reading of, for example, Baggerman, Arianne and Dekker, Rudolf. 2009. *Child of the Enlightenment*. Trans. D. Webb. Leiden: Brill, might suggest the extent to which the text can be read as offering a reductive account of rationalism and its relationship to doubt, the 'subjective' and the 'emotional' within the history of the philosophy of education in the West. For more on this see also Barney, Richard. 1999. *Plots of Enlightenment: Education and the novel in eighteenth century England*. Palo Alto: Stanford.

8. For a classic account of the problem of division on these terms, see Felman, Shoshona. 2003. *Writing and madness (literature/philosophy/psychoanalysis)*. Palo Alto: Stanford University Press, especially pp. 144–164.
9. See Cocks (2009) for a detailed reading of appeals to freedom and the natural within contemporary theories of education. Counter to the notion that all educational theory that does not work within 'radical humanist' discourse is bound by a concern with the 'subjective', the argument here is that the majority of educational theory, 'radical humanist' included, can be read in terms of a commitment to the idea of the self-evidence of the learning subject.
10. Conversely, *The Dangerous Rise* claims that 'our political and philosophical objections to therapeutic education are usually ignored' and that there are 'frequent accusations that we are "uncaring", that we advocate the repression of feelings and a return to the days when children were "seen and not heard", that we tell people to "get over it, get a grip"' (Ecclestone and Hayes 2009, p. 159). Although I would contend that Hayes's call to 'grow up, get a grip' makes it clear where such accusations come from, my interest is not in replicating the opposition between thought and feeling utilised in the arguments that *The Dangerous Rise* claims are levelled against it, nor their reliance upon speculative biography.
11. As will be read in the next chapter, this is repeated in the self-declared 'postmodernity' of arguments put forward by Nigel Thrift.
12. For a comparable reading of issues with O'Neill's logic, see Julia Sklar on the ironically titled 'Stepford Student' webpage: 'If freedom of speech is to be recognised, then it must come hand in hand with freedom to protest... A person has as much right to protest an opinion as another has to voice that opinion in the first place. That's sort of the point, and it's part of what makes open debate so exciting. How dare you accuse us of trying to shut it down. To Brendan O'Neill: You may not agree with what we say, nor how we say it. But for god's sake defend our right to take a stance'. Sklar, Julia. 2016. The unsanctionable nature of protest. http://www.thestepfordstudent.co.uk/the-unsanctionable-nature-of-protest-why-brendan-oneill-is-the-true-enemy-of-freedom-of-speech/. Accessed 4 November 2016.

13. For a criticism of this position, see Leathwood, Carole and Read, Barbara. 2008. *The changing face of higher education: A feminized future*. Berkshire: Open University Press, p. 131.
14. Could the 'eminent sociologist' possibly be Frank Furedi?
15. As indicated previously, ex-members of The Revolutionary Communist Party and contributors to *Living Marxism* have been accused of being reluctant to acknowledge their links, most famously by George Monbiot and Nick Cohen. See Monibiot, George. 2003. Invasion of the entryists. *The Guardian*, 9 December. Cohen, Nick. 2006. Double entryism. *New Humanist*. http://blog.newhumanist.org.uk/2007/01/nick-cohen-vs-institute-of-ideas.html. Accessed 4 November 2016. As The Institute of Ideas and Sense About Science are invested in open debate, the idea that there are unacknowledged connections between its advocates becomes significant. *Spiked!* refutes the accusation of entryism, with Furedi's views on this can be read in Brendan O'Neill. Humanising politics is my only agenda. www.spiked-online.com/newsite/article/3132. Accessed 4 November 2016.

References

AFAF. 2015. http://www.afaf.org.uk/about/. Accessed 5 November 2016

Burman, Erica. 2008. *Deconstructing developmental psychology* (2nd edn). London: Routledge.

Ecclestone, Kathryn, and Dennis Hayes. 2009. *The dangerous rise of therapeutic education*. London: Routledge.

Ellis, Frank. 2010. A curriculum of errors. *The Salisbury Review*. https://issuu.com/salisburyreview/docs/autumn_2010_short_blue. Accessed 6 November 2016.

Guldberg, Helene. 2008. Don't outlaw boisterous banter in the playground. *Spiked! Online*. http://www.spiked-online.com/newsite/article/5928#.WB8nwNSLQdA. Accessed 6 November 2016.

Hayes, Dennis. 2004. Being bullied? Just grow up! *Times Education Supplement*, August 13.

Hayes, Dennis. 2008. For 'post-modern', read 'anti-human'. *Times Education Supplement*, March 31.

Hayes, Dennis. 2010. Decade of success. *Times Higher Education Supplement*, February 25.

Leathwood, Carole, and Barbara Read. 2008. *The changing face of higher education: A feminized future*. Berkshire: Open University Press.

O'Neill, Brendan. 2014. Free speech is so last century. Today's students want the 'right to be comfortable'. *The Spectator*, November 22.

O'Neill, Brendan. 2016. From no platform to safe space: A crisis of enlightenment. In *Unsafe space: The crisis of free speech on campus*, ed. Tom Slater, 22–33. Basingstoke: Palgrave.

CHAPTER 4

New-Managerial Ontology: Materiality, Vision and Disclosure in *Non-Representational Theory* by Nigel Thrift

Abstract Nigel Thrift's *Non-Representational Theory* is a celebration of materiality and flux in postmodern theory and contemporary managerial culture. For Thrift, the idea of 'meaning' is understood to get in the way of the truth of the world: better to creatively engage 'the bare bones of actual occasions'. This Chapter claims that Thrift's arguments are premised upon total clarity of community and communication, despite their commitment to indeterminacy. Indeed, 'non-representational theory' is taken to be indicative of what Jan de Vos names 'the ossification of the social', a seemingly radical anti-humanism that promises access to the objective real. The lack of concern with constitutive frames to be read here provides a possible link between Thrift's academic writing and the new-managerialism he championed as Vice-Chancellor at Warwick.

Keywords Nigel Thrift · Affect · Non-representational theory

1 Reading the VC

In the previous chapter, Katherine Ecclestone and Dennis Hayes were understood to promote the university as a site of a textual certainty, an understanding challenged in this present book through the return of a notion of reading to Higher Education discourse. There is, I argue, a textual indeterminacy that must be repressed in order for authoritative

© The Author(s) 2017
N. Cocks, *Higher Education Discourse and Deconstruction*,
Palgrave Critical University Studies,
DOI 10.1007/978-3-319-52983-7_4

meaning to be secured. It is for this reason that 'radical humanist' claims to intellectual daring require re-examination. In attempting to get safely to the point of danger, issues of language must be bypassed, this resulting in an inability to work through various enabling contradictions.

In this final chapter, I turn to the work of Nigel Thrift, a theorist whose promotion of the 'postmodern' within Higher Education might seem to position him against 'radical humanism'. As in certain arguments forwarded by Diane Purkiss, however, I understand this work to be premised on an appeal to the indisputably 'real'. Indeed, of all the theorists addressed in this present book, Thrift is perhaps the most clearly committed to a materialist world view. The future of education is claimed to rest with physicality rather than textuality: the successful academic institution is one that harnesses the power of both objecthood and embodied feelings, embracing the pre-cognitive, corporeal and indeterminate.

I take Nigel Thrift's work as my focus for three reasons. Firstly, as indicated earlier, he is, in my understanding, the most unapologetic exponent of the kind of postmodern education that is questioned in the work of, for example, John Guillory, Gregory Smulewicz-Zucker, Stefen Collini, Michael Thomson, and Hayes and Ecclestone.[1] Do their concerns have validity, or is Thrift 'alert to the criticisms intellectualists will bring against' his thesis to the extent that he is able to offer a convincing counter narrative? (Thrift 2008, back cover endorsement) Secondly, Thrift was, of course, until recently Vice-Chancellor at Warwick University, and was criticised in this office for his managerial approach, areas of contention including: the suspension of colleagues critical of his rule; a £42,000 yearly pay increase during a period of decreased departmental funding; £80,000 spent on a corporate rebranding exercise; the institution of work casualisation programmes, including the ill-fated TeachHigher initiative; the privileging of expensive research; support for police violence against student protestors; lobbying for Warwick to be exempt from the Freedom of Information Act; and the widely lampooned Warwick style guide.[2] How might Thrift's academic support for postmodernity relate to such policies?[3] Is there a tension between managerial practice and the 'radical' politics championed in Thrift's academic work, or are they mutually supportive? Thirdly, Thrift's understanding of the postmodern is opposed to my own, challenging as he does the discursivity that I take to be of such importance. Engaging his work through a sustained and detailed reading will help define what I understand to be the danger of sidelining questions of textuality in critical and educational theory.

2 NIGEL THRIFT, POSTMODERNITY AND NEW MANAGERIALISM

Nigel Thrift differs from many contemporary theorists of Higher Education in his willingness to defend managerial culture. In 'The Rise of Soft Capitalism', for example, Thrift's landmark essay of 1997, there is a claim to resist academic dismissal of business practice. Central to his argument is an account of a societal move from an 'Isaiah' to a 'Genesis structure'. In the former, the appeal is to a single, correct, God's-eye view of reason that transcends the way humans (or indeed any other things) think, and which promotes the idea of a world that is 'centrally organised, rigidly bounded, and hysterically concerned with impenetrable boundaries' (Thrift 1997, p. 31, quoting Kenneth Jowitt). Counter to this, a 'Genesis structure' sets out 'a view of the world in which knowledge has become an archipelago of islands of epistemic stability in a sea of disorder, fluctuations, noise, randomness and chaos' (Thrift 1997, p. 32). Thrift's contention is that this 'postmodern' condition is also that of contemporary 'new-managerial' culture. Indeed, academic work informed by postmodernity 'share[s] many…concerns' with contemporary business (Thrift 1997, p. 30). Not only are both understood to reject stagnancy, but they also require embodied and practical forms of knowing, 'knowledge that cannot be written down and packaged', and the promotion of 'supple institutional structures' (Thrift 1997, p. 30). It is odd, then, claims Thrift, that critical theory is so dismissive of managerialism. Rather than engaging points of convergence, those working in the humanities and social sciences tend to rely upon a limited idea of capitalism, generalising it into:

> an all-pervasive cultural formation, usually through its migration into the symbolic realm. Capitalism can be elevated into something so self-evident that it can be brought on whenever a connective explanation is called for. Or Capitalism becomes a reading, which can then be made into a transcendental haunting, both everywhere and nowhere. (Thrift 1997, p. 29)

For Thrift, this ignores the potentialities in new iterations of capitalism, the way in which community exchange systems, for example, might be turned against existing systems of oppression (Thrift 1997, p. 52). Standardised accounts of capitalism fail to recognise the possibility of 'pleasure' and subversion within the new, 'soft', postmodern form of business (Thrift 1997, p. 40). Lest this be read as naïve, Thrift claims to recognise also the 'hard-edge' to such practices. Workers will lose their jobs, and managers will be overworked and may become cynical (Thrift 1997, pp. 50–52). However, we should not be convinced by too trenchant criticism. As Thrift explains in *Non-Representational Theory*, the tendency to focus on the edge not only results in a limited understanding of the reality of the contemporary moment, and the subversive possibilities it offers, it is also an expression of unrecognised privilege:

> [t]he social sciences and humanities suffer from a certain kind of over-theorization at present. There are too many theories, all of them seemingly speaking on behalf of those whose lives have been damaged by the official structures of power. A cynic might think that the profusion of 'fast' theories created by academies is simply a mirror of the rise of brainy classes, who are able to live a life of permanent theoretical revolution whilst everyone else does the dirty work. That would be too harsh. But the criticism is not therefore without any force at all. (Thrift 2008, p. 3)

There is a scale of theorisation, it would seem, one that is tipped by work concerned with those adversely affected by power structures. The 'cynic' might be wrong in their estimation of such work, but not completely. For Thrift, academics are not tasked with speaking truth to power. Such speech is, in fact, a power to which further speech must be directed. After all, 'most of the angst in the new-managerialist discourse is produced by and for the middle class – not the working class' (Thrift 1997, p. 50).[4]

At this early stage, and even before what I take to be the problematic geography of the 'hard edge' is worked through in any detail, it is worth addressing this final point. Here, for example, is an alternative account from Chris Lorenz:

> In view of the chronic problems created by [New Public Management] for the ('elitist') academic profession it is not surprising that ('democratic') political support for it has been entirely dependent on [Value For Money] ideology and corresponding spending cuts in public services that could be sold to the taxpayer as income tax cuts. This has been the neoliberals' most powerful tactic in generating public support for NPM, and this explains why public sector cuts through constant improvements in efficiency are a permanent feature of NPM. The imperative to cut spending (thou shalt reduce costs) has not, on the other hand, held managers back from awarding themselves salaries at some presumed market rate. This is possible because

under NPM managers do not have to hold themselves accountable to anyone other than themselves. (Lorenz, 2012, p. 614)

The suggestion here is that Thrift's move to limit the effects of managerialism to the angsty middle-classes is problematic, as such effects are part of a wider discourse of austerity. Moreover, in light of the controversies surrounding Thrift's salary increases, the long-standing debate concerning the living wage under his rule, and his institution's utilisation of zero-hours contracts, what Lorenz has to say about inequality in employment and the related lack of accountability can be understood to have a bearing on the historic situation at Warwick.[5] It could also be argued that such inequality is repeated across the sector, and is often realised in even more dramatic fashion, with universities, under the instruction of hugely expensive consultancies, enacting restructuring programmes that first target non-academic staff, an operation that has occurred in some instances immediately after the de-recognition of unions. I would contend, therefore, that in both the specific case of Higher Education and in the wider operations of public services, the claim that managerialism impacts on a discrete, privileged section of society is at least highly contentious.[6]

Both the dismissal of a middle class, academic critique of managerial culture within universities and the excitement regarding the intellectual implications of business culture, are developed in later work, published after Thrift had been appointed Vice-Chancellor at Warwick. In what follows I will be focusing on 'Afterwords', an extended chapter in the most celebrated of these, *Non-Representational Theory*.[7] The chapter has been chosen as it is described as 'an attempt to make a definitive statement about non-representational theory...' (Thrift 2008, p. 24). The eleven years that have elapsed since 'The Rise of Soft Capitalism' have introduced a shift within this theory, however. Whereas in 1997 Thrift was addressing individual human subjects, story-telling, and the formative nature of discourse, by 2008 all this is rejected, a concern with 'a notion of meaning involving symbols that are constitutive of the world' having given way to an investment in 'the lived immediacy of actual experience, before any reflection on it' (Thrift 2008, p. 6). The postmodernity to be celebrated is one producing 'a poetics of the unthought, of...a well-structured pre-reflective world which, just because it lacks explicit articulation, is not therefore without grip' (Thrift 2008, p. 16). It follows that Thrift is cautious of endorsing Sheldon Wolin's claim that 'high-technology, globalised capitalism is radically incongruent with democracy', attacking as he does 'the orthodox politics of resentment of left radicalism which has become an increasingly sterile political repertoire whose appeals to unity simply repeat the old terms of succession within a foreclosed "radical" community intent on the pleasures of victimization' (Thrift 2008, p. 3). Thrift is instead 'searching for another way of going on', and this consists of:

> a microbiopolitics of the subliminal, much of which operates in the half-second delay between action and cognition, a microbiopolitics which understands the kind of biological-cum-cultural gymnastics that take place in this realm which is increasingly susceptible to new and sometimes threatening knowledges and technologies that operate upon it in ways that produce effective outcomes, even when the exact reasons may be opaque, a micropolitics which understands the insufficiency of argument to political life without, however, denying its pertinence. (Thrift 2008, p. 192)

As such, I read Thrift to position himself within what has become known as the 'turn to affect', a movement that arguably remains the dominant force in contemporary critical theory.[8] Most famously advocated by Brian Massumi, engaged with Evolutionary Psychology and Performance Studies, and citing as its influences the work of Gilles Deleuze, Silvan Tomkins, Baruch Spinoza and Alfred North Whitehead amongst others, this is a philosophy that rejects what it sees as an undue stress on meaning and cognition, preferring to focus on all that must be in place for a rationalist mastery to convince itself of its sufficiency.[9]

In a rare questioning account, Ruth Leys takes to task the leading advocates in the field, Thrift included:

> the disconnect between 'ideology' and affect produces as one of its consequences a relative indifference to the role of ideas and beliefs in politics, culture, and art in favour of an 'ontological' concern with different people's corporeal affective reactions. (Leys 2011, p. 451)[10]

It could be argued that Thrift's aforementioned statement concerning 'microbiopolitics' is 'alert to the criticisms intellectualists will bring', as it makes clear his understanding of the 'pertinence' of argument, this in keeping with the claim that non-representational theory is a 'modest supplement' only to wider political discourse (Thrift 2008, p. 20). In my reading, however, this is belied by a repeated insistence upon a clear distinction between the linguistic and the worldly, condemning, for example, any attempt to 'overtly textualise nondiscursive somatic experience', arguing that 'the body "is not about signs and meanings but about a mechanics of space"', and suggesting that a political future is only to be secured if we '["perhaps"] stop talking and start dancing' (Thrift 2008, p. 149, quoting Richard Shusterman). This, then, is an understanding of what the 'pertinence' of discourse is: a desire for it to stop.[11]

Here it might be worth reading through one instance of what I take to be this inconsistent construction of the text and the world in a little more detail. At one stage, for example, there is a condemnation of 'the vapid certainties of so much current cultural work' that 'consider[s] life from the point of view of individual agents who generate action' rather than that intent on 'weaving a poetic of the common practices and skills which produce people, selves and worlds'. Counter to this, at another stage, the insistence is that:

> I hold to a sense of *personal authorship*, no matter that the trace is very faint and no matter that the brain is a society, different parts of which are dynamically and differentially connected to all manner of environments. And the reason? Because how things seem is often more important than what they are:
> 'The fact is that it seems to each of us that we have a conscious will. It seems we have selves. It seems we have minds. It seems we are agents. It seems we cause what we do. Although it is sobering and ultimately accurate to call this an illusion, it is a mistake to think the illusory is trivial.' (Thrift 2008, pp. 112, 13, quoting Daniel Wegner)

Certainly, a conflict can be read here between this statement and Thrift's questioning account of 'current cultural work': the triviality of illusion is rejected within the dismissal of the 'vapid certainties' of contemporary theory, yet 'often' it is the most important thing there is. In other words, if at one stage an ontological interest in 'the direct significances of practices' holds sway, at another it is the derided 'contemplative world' that is privileged (Thrift 2008, pp. 113, 65, 66). The quotation concerning 'personal authorship' does not simply side with subjectivity, however. A privileging of individual perspective can indeed be read in so far as 'importan[ce]' is a matter for 'each of us', a native experience, an aspect of the seeming that acts as a counter to 'what is'. Despite this, importance is also beyond 'how things seem', relying on the other that falls outside 'seeming', the 'how things are' that is the fact of the brain being a society, or whatever. And it follows that if the native experience of 'each of us' is what is of importance, it is the case from a narrative point of view that is both one of 'us' suffering illusions, and that other that knows the fact of this suffering for what it is, a fact also available to the additional subject positions necessarily residing in the category 'each of us'. Subjectivity does not keep to its right place, dependent as it is on its other for its very being. It is a problem that can be read from the other direction, as importance is also 'often' something other than 'what [things] are': as importance is constituted as relational, it cannot wholly lodge with either side. Importance is both native and an excess to this. It problematises the strict opposition between fact and impression that Thrift's argument has occasion to require.

Such a binary structure can itself be read to be a wider problem for *Non-Representational Theory*, as, in keeping with 'the affective turn', Thrift understands his analysis to counter the oppositional logic that would separate 'seeming' and 'being': the 'link' between 'account and reality... has been dissolved away' (Thrift 2008, p. 110). It could be argued, however, that the move to disrupt 'the typical dualistic reduction of ontology to epistemology' cannot help but restore the binary. Thrift's argument here expresses a desire to escape the perceived shortcomings of a cultural theory dependent upon a 'constructionist notion of the body as simply an inscribed surface... a static signified to be filled with signs of society... divorced from other things' (Thrift 2008, p. 61). Within this argument, the derided theory is taken to fail to recognise the force of the other, the fact of the object that acts upon and within ostensibly 'subjective' knowledge. In the words of Sue Walsh, however, from her recent critique of contemporary theories of embodiment, there is a 'recuperation' of the prior real in Thrift's formulation, a repetition of the opposition under question: there is, after all, a claim to an ontology that can indeed be separated from an epistemology, a thing known to be other than construction (Walsh 2015, pp. 20–36). But from what position is such a separation to be known?

As Thrift's argument is premised upon the rejection of textuality, such difficulties can be understood to fall outside the scope of study set out within *Non-Representational Theory*. Counter to this, I am suggesting that it is only through a reading of the terms of Thrift's text that the binary logic can be disrupted, with the subjective constituted by its other even at the point of their apparent separation. Thrift's dismissal of 'textualism', of the 'transient features' of 'narratibility, and 'close third-person explanation' means such collapse is not to be engaged (Thrift 2008, p. 69).

For Thrift then, what escapes in any given instance is always only the purity of the real, with this understood, somehow, as the necessary condition for any questioning of oppositional thinking. I take Ruth Leys to address the difficulty of this logic when she criticises '[t]he new-affect theorists' tendency to reject psychoanalysis or try to reconceptualise it in materialist-technological terms', as 'in the process of revising and amending and materializing Freud, they end up abandoning the notion of the... unconscious. On this post-psychoanalytic model, what is not fully conscious must necessarily be corporeal or material' (Leys 2011, p. 459). In turning from questions of language, I take Thrift's move to repress the difference necessary to meaning. Within his arguments, what opposes the self, or consciousness, or meaning, can only be a lost, and thus redeemable, real, never an impossible, formative, and irredeemable textuality.[12]

Even in 1997, however, within the supportive reading of the discursive, a comparative difficulty in working through the tension between the text and the world can be read:

> [rationalities are based on] a notion of meaning involving symbols which are constitutive of the world and not just mirrors of it; and reliant on categories that are not independent of the world but are defined by mental processes (like metaphor, metonymy and mental imaging) -processes which mean that there can be no objectively correct description of reality. (Thrift 1997, p. 32)

I read this to be a more nuanced account than that offered earlier, at least in so far as the concern is with a world constituted by symbols, rather than an ontology fixed upon 'extra-textual practice' (Thrift 2008, p. 132). In this understanding, the world cannot be separated from a discourse located 'within the site of culture', to borrow a formulation from Judith Butler (Butler 1988, p. 524). For Thrift, at this stage, 'categories' are not independent of a world constituted by symbols, and this dependence arises from their definition by mental processes. The claim might then be that mental processes are constituted by symbols, with the symbolic therefore subject to its own operations. On these terms, metonymy, for example, is not only that which brings the world to meaning but an aspect of the world that springs forth from the symbolic, lacking any 'objective' status.

Certainly, metonymy is not free from its own logic within Thrift's formulation, as, for example, along with metaphor and mental imaging, it is itself metonymically linked to mental processes. I am appealing to something more than this, however, the threat of a symbolic that does not keep to its proper place, and in this fails to act as the guarantor of a transitive world. It is a threat that runs counter to a reading of Thrift's quotation that takes the embodied physicality of 'mental processes' to be that which secures categories as other than 'objectively correct'. 'Mental processes', in this understanding, are temporal and locatable, and it is this that makes them worldly. It is necessary, then, for such processes to stand outside of any symbolic register. There is, in short, a difficulty in placing mental processes within the claim that there can be 'no objective correct description'.

As evidenced previously, it is my contention that this is not an isolated problem: I understand the 'objective[ly] correct' to consistently return to Thrift's argument. Despite the claim that only a concern with objecthood, the biological, and the immediacy of emotion can truly lead to an 'anti-subtantialist' understanding of the world, the flux and uncertainty that Thrift sets so much store by can, in his analysis, always be known for the pre-discursive reality of existence they truly are, this, moreover, from what Jan de Vos has termed a point of 'zero level subjectivity': the truth of existence is not known by any particular subject, but from a non-position of unaccountable mastery, this a 'hegemonic discourse which serves both as a tool to lay bare real life and to allow us to take the outsider position'.[13]

I find it helpful to introduce Jan de Vos's writing on neo-liberalism and globalisation at this stage as, within his questioning account, I take criticisms of 'psychologization' to encounter comparable difficulties to those met by *Non-Representational Theory* in its dismissal of cultural investments in the subject, as introduced earlier. For de Vos, if dominant forms of psychology 'promise...to open the door to something we have lost; a more genuine and authentic presence with ourselves and the world', then 'critique of psychologisation' can be understood to ironically 'promise the same thing...i.e. a grasp of the world, the others and yourself delivered through revealing what they are really, really about...' (de Vos 2012, pp. 2–3). De Vos concludes that there is an 'ossification of the social' when positioned against the psychological, and this:

> is realized by a whole array of psy-approaches, all result[ing] in the objectification and the turning of subjectivity in a thingness, be it genes,

neurotransmitters, evolutionary patterns, emotions, skills, brain areas, childhood traumas, cognitions, rapid eye movements... Each is a commodity in the psycho-political economy. (de Vos 2012, p. 119)

It is my claim that, in its fixation upon a 'world of things... that have their own resonances', *Non-Representational Theory* repeats such an ossifying and commodifying move, joining 'the shared fantasy... that there is an access to unmediated and direct life, life as it is' (de Vos 2012, p. 99).[14] If Thrift sets up the rejection of subjectivity as a radical alternative to naïve humanist investment in the individual, it can also be understood as a resistance to a working through of the difficulty of subjectivity, the impossibility of it being either fully realised or dismissed, and the political questions of positionality, otherness and difference it requires. For de Vos:

> The dissemination of theories on the functioning of the brain, social skills, group dynamics, etc., seems to bring us back to meaningful, manageable life-world: denying the late-modern alienation of globalisation it thrives on the illusion that Real Life lurks just behind the veils of post-modern complexity... here the link between certain tendencies within mainstream psy-praxis and the populist conservative discourses becomes thin as they share the same envisioning of a lost but regainable authentic, pastoral kind of first life. (de Vos 2012, p. 136)

It is my contention that *Non-Representational Theory* offers an evidence-based practice that is resistant to understanding its own positionality. It does not credit its own interventions. In claiming access to the world as it is, Thrift requires the repression of reading, as it can be understood to trouble the notion of an objective real. Such a rejection is not taken to be an aspect of the operation of the hard edge of capitalism, however, and as such *Non-Representational Theory* is unable to work through what I take to be constitutive difficulties with the new managerialism it claims to soberly assess: its resistance to the discursive; what Kathleen Lynch describes as the 'façade of certainty that makes it relatively unassailable'; the repression of the frame necessary to its audit (Lynch 2015, p. 190). The result is that for Thrift, the threat of the managerial 'hard-edge' can be managed and mastered. The edge is located, and thus free from the risk of *pharmakon*, as analysed in Chapter 1 of this present book. *That* would indeed be a constitutive risk, one impossible to corral in any safe and permanent sense. For Thrift, on the other hand, the 'hard-edge' is always known, expressed in such local phenomena as job cuts and managerial stress, and can thus be thrown out from the main body, leaving the micro-management and transparency that remains free from taint.

3   '[...] A Space for my Father [...]'

Following the analysis of Ruth Leys, my contention is that, despite its various appeals to indeterminacy and fluidity, *Non-Representational Theory* repeatedly calls upon an absence that can be returned wholly to knowledge, a sensation or object always prior to language and cognition that can be known on its own terms. I am interested in thinking through this appeal to a recoverable real in more detail, and to this end turn now to the opening lines of 'Afterwords', as here Thrift confronts what he takes to be our culture's undue investment in language and cognition through an account of his own experience of loss:

> This chapter is connected with a particular event, the death of my father. I feel a need to write the event and yet, as I make clear in this chapter, I am not at all sure that is what I want to do. In a sense, I believe that this writing down is a part of the problem. I do not want to take over my father's being by making him into fodder for yet more interpretation, by colonizing his traces.
> Why? Because my father was a good man who did a lot of good; more than most, I suspect. Almost nothing he ever did was written down and whereas I once would have seen this as a problem I now think that putting his life in order through text ... may ... be just another form of condescension. (Thrift 2008, p. 109)

We might begin with the understanding that 'my father' is prior to writing: his death is an established event yet to be written, that has nothing to do with the written. Writing, it would seem, has certain ill effects. In writing I would be wanting to colonise 'my father's' traces, making his being 'fodder for yet more interpretation'. The concern here, in part, is for 'my father' to be protected from transformation and iteration. Within this formulation there is no need to engage 'interpretation' in any way other than the fact of its continuum; the more that is to come cannot be differentiated from that which has passed. Interpretation knows no difference, a sterile sameness also to be read in the notion of 'fodder' upon which the repetition is founded. Here the danger is also one of alteration rather iteration, however: 'my father' is not understood as an end in himself, but a colonised subject made into something other than himself. One difficulty at this stage is that 'my father' is always of necessity in this condition. He is 'my father', after all; narrated from a point of view other than his own; a relational identity. What is to be protected, moreover, is a 'being' that is owned by, yet other than, 'my father', and 'traces' likewise owned, while 'writing down' is not an act upon his trace but a 'making him' into something other. The assumption is that within the pre-linguistic realm there is no significant difference between 'my father', 'him', 'his being' or 'his traces'. I read 'my father' thus to be caught up in a 'transcendental haunting, both everywhere and nowhere', to borrow a phrase from Thrift.

The advantage to Thrift's argument of what I take to be such a 'haunting' can be further read as the introduction to 'Afterwords' progresses:

> I am not sure, in other words, that he needs writing down, or, put in another way, we need a form of writing that can disclose and value his legacy – the somatic currency of bodily stances he passed on, the small sayings and large generosities, and, in general, his stance to the world – in such a way as to make it less important for him to be written. (Thrift 2008, p. 109)

Despite the uncertainty as to what 'he' needs, there is no doubt that such needs are at stake, and that 'he' is not in a position to guarantee what they might be: needs require another to identify and meet them. When 'put in another way', however, the interest is not in what 'he needs', but in the disclosure and valuing of 'his legacy'. Here, the pronoun might be understood to fall outside what is valued and disclosed: this is not about the failure to write down a 'he', but the demand to bring a particular 'legacy' to light. This is an investment in a detached, material instance as the legacy is identified as 'the somatic currency of bodily stances he passed on'. The 'he' is located in the past, and other to the physical 'bodily stances' that persist. These stances are not limited to a particular, owned body, but can be taken up by any other. As what is passed on is 'his stance *to* the world' [my italics], however, there is an excess necessary to their limit, although such a formulation only goes so far in undoing the opposition between the body and its seeming other, as 'his stance' is necessarily not of 'the world'.[15] There is a further excess, of course, as what is passed on is '*his* stance to the world', a bequest impossible to realise [my italics]. This is the difficulty with 'legacy': if in one sense, the inheritance requires 'my father's' absence, it is a lack that confers ownership, and in this stages a ghostly return. In so far as I am to take up the 'stance' of 'my father', he is an irrelevance, yet in disappearing from the scene he becomes its master, this stance I adopt never truly being mine, but a trace of my father that, at one stage, is interchangeable with what it mourns. Unlike the deathly repetition of interpretation, legacy is taken to call upon difference, generation, history; the persistence of the father in the other and in his absence. Within this argument, legacy does not require any understanding of this passing down, as it is known to exist prior to any disclosure or valuing of it, and this again because it must, in its central, independent truth, at all costs resist the repetition of interpretation, the excess of writing. Within Thrift's argument, there can be nothing linguistic about this legacy, even as it consists of 'small sayings'.

The failure to work through such ironies of language and legacy can be further read in the following formulation:

> As I work up a non-representationalist style of work that I hope can describe and value this legacy, this thought lies constantly at the back of my mind. Sometimes, we go into a man's study and find his books and papers all over the place, and say without hesitation: 'What a mess!... Yet, at other times we may go into a room which looks very like the first, but after looking around we decide that we must leave it just as it is, recognising that, in this case, even the dust has its place...'
>
> How, then, might we find a space for my father? This is the question I want to ask in this chapter. But to ask it requires a consideration of the politics of what [Peggy] Phelan calls the 'unmarked', that, is, an attempt to find, value and retain what is not marked as 'here', yet palpably still reverberates; invisible dust still singing and dancing. Phelan approaches this question of disappearance from a psychoanalytic perspective. As will become clear, my approach is a rather different one, based on valuing practices in and for themselves... As she puts it 'by locating the subject in what cannot be reproduced within the ideology of the visible, I am attempting to revalue a belief in subjectivity and identity which is not visibly represented' (Thrift 2008, pp. 109–110, quoting Wittgenstein and Peggy Phelan).

A simple opposition might be understood to be at work here, one between leaving or not leaving things as they are, yet such an assessment discounts further oppositions, for example that between saying without hesitation and a decision that is unsaid. The latter occurs after 'looking around', whereas the lack of hesitation in the former is the result of not looking in this way: we merely go into a man's study; any idea concerning the look of the place is introduced only with the second room 'which looks very like the first'. Speech is thus the occasion for a failure to hesitate, look and decide. According to the narration, however, all of this is a 'thought', one that 'lies constantly in the back of my mind', and the thought, moreover, is a quotation, as the words within quotation marks are acknowledged as Wittgenstein's. The difficulty here is not only that the failure to articulate that is positioned against the instantaneous is constituted within language, but that thought itself is taken to be textual. In taking up the non-representational style, there is a thought that would seem to call for language to be bypassed, a thought that is located as an object, there in the back of my mind, yet one that is also in this the language of another.

Such an understanding runs counter to the notion of language as secondary read in the resistance to putting 'life in order through text'. Here, on the other hand, '[w]hat a mess!' applies to certain men whose rooms provoke an unhesitant verbal response, rooms that are not to be left as they are, thus failing to offer 'legacy'. This can be understood to run counter to the philosophy of the half-second delay: the valuing of 'legacy' requires hesitation, and thus is not to be found in 'microbiopolitics of the subliminal'. The hesitation results in the recognition that the rooms of other men do not need tidying up, and this is because they are already in order: everything has 'its place'. Rather than located only within the secondary site of text, order is claimed to be prior to interpretation: there is a natural order to the world, and it should not be disturbed. Despite this, the claim that 'even the dust has its place' suggests, in relation to the question of 'my father', a problem with the notion of a primary realm that should not suffer intervention, as dust, in my reading, signals a lack of disturbance, and as such is not original, not simply part of the native world of 'my father'. If the dust is to figure the passage of time, then the mark of preservation is included in what is preserved. There is a further difficulty, however, as the validation of the place of dust leads to a question concerning the finding of 'a space for my father'. As it is to be 'found', space can be read as existing prior to the finding. It is not my father's space when found, as it is *for* my father. This suggests, perhaps, that at one time, my father is understood not to occupy a space. I take the space that is found not only to be empty but to persist in this condition, even when understood to be for the father: the space is never compromised as a space by being 'for my father'. There is a tension, then, between the demand to value the place of the object and the claim that my father should be granted a space, yet does not require it, and, when in receipt of it, does not affect it. If my father transcends space, at one stage, there is something, at least, that remains present, with the goal of Thrift's analysis being 'to find, value and retain what is not marked as "here", yet palpably still reverberates; invisible dust still singing and dancing'. For Thrift, the error is in the 'mark[ing]', with 'here' placed within quotation marks, a linguistic rather than a 'real' location. I read the claim to invisibility to repeat this move: Thrift understands the problem of the visible and the marked to be that of the 'represented'. The 'palpable' is thus 'non-representational': the dust is in its correct place, and the truth of this can simply be felt. One additional difficulty with this argument is that it is set against the 'look[ing] around' that leads to the recognition of the correct place of dust.

In all of this, I understand *Non-Representational Theory* to be caught between an investment in presence and in absence, in physicality and transcendence. This is, in one sense, Thrift's calling card, his claim to the importance of the non-representative 'style', his privileging of the 'active presence of absent things', the sense in which such 'an emphasis on things questions the solidity of the world' (Thrift 2008, pp. 10, 120). In my reading, however, the formulations on offer are inconsistent rather than problematizing. Thus I understand Thrift's interest in the real to require 'look[ing]', and the fixity of place, yet the resistance to epistemology demands an accessible existence that does not hang on cognition or visualisation. Likewise, both Thrift's rejection of naïve humanism and his interest in the persistence of the father, require the latter's location in the material trace, yet the demand for legacy necessitates the father transcend any given object. To reformulate: the commitment to materiality requires what Thrift terms a 'distributed ecology of thought' necessitating, in my reading, the 'ossification of the social' and the objectification of the 'subjective' (Thrift 2008, p. 59). For Thrift, the 'stance' of 'my father' can be taken up by another as it is a pure, material instance, yet this comes with the unlooked for implication that 'my father' might be wholly available to vision, and therefore located somewhere other than the 'microbiopolitics of the subliminal' with its rejection of 'the ideology of the visible'.[16]

4   Disclosure

In my understanding, then, there are occasions when *Non-Representational Theory*'s 'valu[ing of] practices in and of themselves' necessitates an absence of vision. According to Thrift, singing and dancing are not for the eye, and are not, of course, to be discussed. They cannot even be thought. All such operations will leave their mark, and marking will alter practice (Thrift 2008, p. 137). Calling on the work of Fred Newman and Lois Holzman, Thrift claims that in order to institute a form of retention that would remain 'unmarked':

> 'we must substantively eliminate the substantive myths of modernism (amongst them the individuated mind, the individual self, and individual cognitions) only as we deconstructively/reconstructively (socially activistically) eliminate the mythic ancient (Aristotelian) *forms* of modernism (explaining, describing, interpreting, identifying, and knowing).' (Thrift 2008, p. 122, quoting Fred Newman and Lois Holzman)

This is to be achieved through a 'third kind' of knowledge, one that 'gives up modern assumptions about... the orderliness of the world' and 'argues that the world is constructed through activity, especially the activity of talk', this understood not to be 'primarily communication (or ruled governed and concerned with exchanging meanings)' (Thrift 1997, p. 122). For Thrift, knowledge is produced within the movement of action, not retrospectively constructed, a 'knowing from within a situation... rather than knowing-what or knowing-how, it is "knowledge-in-practice" and "knowledge held in common with others"' (Thrift 1997, p. 122).

According to this argument, 'action' allows for an understanding of a complex world on its own terms. As the analysis offered previously has suggested, however, 'orderliness' is not easily dismissed within *Non-Representational Theory*, invested as it is in a pre-cognitive realm where things have their right place. Indeed, as I will argue, within 'Afterwords' such a right place is what the 'third kind' of managerial knowledge is there to establish.

I will begin here with Thrift's claim that the action of talk is to be 'conceived of as a "structure of presuppositions and expectations of a non-cognitive, gestural kind that unfolds in the temporal movement of joint action"' (Thrift 1997, p. 122, quoting John Shotter). I read the structure so conceived to support the privileging of action over thought, in so far as this structure can be understood to be independent of any thinking subject. This is supported by the dynamic nature of the structure, it is 'of presuppositions...of a gestural kind', and this 'unfolds...' I understand the appeal to the structure to be problematic from the first, however. There is, for example, that within structure that escapes structurality: as 'presuppositions and expectations' are what the structure is 'of', they cannot be wholly confined to such structure. The presuppositions are also constituted by an excess in so far as they are 'of a non-cognitive gestural kind'. The gestural is a variety of structured presupposition, and it is this that 'unfolds'. If again, this confirms the structure's dynamism, it can also be read to ironically construct a discrete structure and gesture that are unfolded, an unfolding, moreover, that is 'in' a 'movement' other than its own, this one 'of joint action'. The difficulty here is that rather than simply reinforcing the dynamic nature of action, the movements realised in other movements introduce the destabilising logic of the supplement to a philosophy of the moment, one that is necessarily resistant to any notion of a constitutive excess. It is Thrift's contention that a commitment to 'the direct significances of practices' results in a 'processual' understanding in which 'there is no last word, only infinite becoming and constant reactivation', yet something is repeatedly falling outside of movement (Thrift 1997, pp. 113–114). This is not simply the difficulty of a seemingly independent moment that has nonetheless been 'conceived of', but an excess to action that returns as its structural requirement.

It is Thrift's contention that the virtue of actions such as 'talk' is that they lead to 'new practices' and these 'can make us more attuned to sensing other possibilities', this the process that, after Charles Spinosa, he names 'disclosure':

> instead of helping us to 'find' or 'discover' something already existing, but supposedly hidden behind appearances [knowledge as practice] help[s] us grasp something new, as yet unseen, that can be sensed in the emerging articulation of the appearances unfolding before our very eyes (or ears). (Thrift 1997, p. 122, quoting Shotter)

Here it might be thought that tensions between structure and process have been addressed: this is not about the uncovering of prior essences, but a radical originality. Again, however, I read a disruptive excess to return to the narrative of dynamism. Despite the distrust of language, appearances are 'articulat[ed]'. This is an 'emerging' articulation, however, and thus one caught up in the movement that is defined against the textual. It is known that the articulation is not complete, yet this lack does not get in the way of identifying what emerges *as* articulation. It is this emerging articulation, rather than any unfolding appearance, 'that can be sensed'. Despite this, it is known that the articulation is of 'appearances'. 'Unfolding' appearances oppose the 'hidden', not only as appearances, but also because what appears is an unfolding, rather than a final revelation. There is no secret to emerge, no 'something already existing... supposedly hidden behind appearances'. For Thrift and Shotter, at this stage, the hidden real is a delusion. Counter to this, what there truly is, what we can 'grasp', is taken to be 'something new as yet unseen', 'sensed in the emerging articulation'. In both cases, 'something' eludes vision, either because it is hidden or unseen, yet one 'something' is falsely 'supposed...', the other genuinely there. The hidden requires an appearance to be positioned behind; a simple spatial arrangement that, I take Thrift to argue, is understood to perpetuate binary thinking. The 'unseen' remains in its condition through a more complex logic: the 'something' is only sensed, and seeing is not included in this sensing, and what is sensed is an articulation of appearances, not an appearance itself, and the appearance anyway is never seen, merely 'unfolding before our eyes'. The 'something' cannot hide behind appearance in this formulation, as appearance is always unseen. The 'yet unseen', on the other hand, does not necessarily have to stay in this condition, yet if seeing were to occur, this would not change the nature of the 'something'. It is there, waiting for a vision. It follows that Thrift's support for the processual, 'anti-substantialist' philosophy is limited. His arguments rely on a 'something' that cannot be questioned, yet can be known and this in a way that cannot be gainsaid, because knowledge is not about meaning or communication, but the inescapably 'palpable'. As such, Thrift's analysis repeats the claim Ruth Leys identifies within affect theory, as discussed earlier: 'disagreement about meaning [is] irrelevant to cultural analysis'.

Crucially, for the arguments within this present book, disagreement about meaning is also understood to be irrelevant to institutional change: Here, for example, is Thrift's account of workplace transformation:

> [t]here are at least three ways that it is possible to change a disclosive space in response to the realization that practices are not in harmony: focusing a dispersed practice (articulation); making what was a marginal practice central (reconfiguration); and adopting and activating neighbouring practice (cross appropriation). Such changes in practice nearly always come

about through involved experimentation rather than deliberative thinking. (Thrift 2008, p. 123)

Within the institution, 'disclosure' allows a 'realisation' that is not dependent on thinking, or, as we have read, on seeing. Instead, a space has disclosed harmony, or its lack, this through the experimentation described earlier as 'joint action'. This is not about individual players, but an action that can be understood to be held by numerous subjects from a position that is not that of any one of them. Disclosure 'comes through' the site of the 'involved', a form of knowing shorn of excess. According to Thrift's own retrospective account, although 'when subsequently written about, [institutional change is] often couched in terms of the deliberative model of going on', this does not reflect the reality of the situation. *Non-Representative Theory* claims to know that it mourns the past moment in a way that does not alter its reality, testifying to the radical independence of the action. My contention is that this is dependent on an 'ossification' of the social: the social is taken to be an objective process that cannot be reduced to any linguistic, secondary or subjective frame, and is thus *radically available*.

I find it helpful at this stage to turn once more to arguments put forward by Bill Readings in *The University in Ruins*.[17] That text concludes with a plea for a 'community of dissensus' based not on a mutual, and wholly communicable understanding of others, but instead on an obligation to the other arising from a lack of complete knowledge (Readings 1996, pp. 188–189). In one sense, the formulation offered by Readings might be taken to repeat Thrift's recognition of an uncompromised otherness: 'we do not know in advance the nature of our obligations to others, obligations that have no origin except in the sheer fact of the existence of Otherness – people, animals, things other to ourselves – that comports an incalculable obligation' (Readings 1996, pp. 188–189). The following passage suggests to me an important distinction, however:

> The social bond is the fact of an obligation to others that we cannot fully understand. We are obligated to them without being able to say exactly why. For if we could say why, if the social bond could be made an object of cognition, then we would not really be dealing with an obligation at all but with a ratio of exchange. If we knew what our obligations were, then we could settle them, compensate them, and be freed from them in return for a payment. (Readings 1996, p. 188)

The focus for Thrift, I would argue, is on the fact of 'cognition': if we could only rid ourselves of thinking, and the false and stable object it requires, the animal or object would be free to carry its own meaning. The aim is to free theory from the tyranny of the subject. As such, *Non-Representational Theory* can claim to appreciate what Readings terms 'things other to ourselves' for what they truly are, this in a radical fashion that gives them 'equal weight, and I do mean equal' (Thrift 2008, p. 9). I would suggest that to argue thus is not to escape the problem Readings identifies, however, but instead to fall into the surety of knowledge that for him signals the end of 'obligation', and thus the gap that grants education its movement, its possibility.[18] Thrift offers certainty, an unproblematic access to the material independence of the other: for Readings 'we can never totally know, finally and exhaustively judge, the other to which we are bound', whereas for Thrift 'objects think', 'things have their own resonances', and these resonances and thoughts can be known absolutely, precisely in so far as they are not bound to the thought of another (Readings 1996, p. 190; Thrift 2008, pp. 60, 117). As I read it, this is an example of what Readings terms the 'self-transparency at the heart of the modernist project': 'the utopia of self-transparency, of a society immediately present to itself in which all members communicate unrestrictedly with all others all of the time and without misunderstanding or delay' (Readings 1996, p. 190). The independence of the other offers the same promise as the 'S-bend' in Diane Purkiss's *agora*, or the truth of the objective world that informs Ecclestone and Hayes's restorationist university. Not only do I understand this 'irresponsible desire to know what it is we encounter in the other' to be problematic on its own terms, but, as has been read earlier, the claim to know from a position of zero-subjectivity, and thus side-step questions of empiricism, is also always compromised (Readings 1996, p. 189). Take, for example, the knots in which Thrift's argument ties itself while trying to evade the demand of the visual: a disclosive space requires the unseen to unfold before our eyes. This has to be: seeing would introduce a cut in the realm of the objective real. But what is such a positioned unfolding without seeing? And what does it mean for this theory of embodiment to dismiss a consideration of seeing? When defending his ontology, after all, Thrift claims that his aim is 'to see the thing itself, to see things as they "merely" are' (Thrift 2008, p. 53).[19] One advantage to the notion of this seeing without seeing is that it lessens the threat of an invasive institution. For Thrift, the ideal working environment is one that grants access to ever smaller sites of 'microbiopolitics'. These cannot, it is argued, be engaged by the subject, or questioned for what they are. This is not a matter of repressive surveillance, Thrift contends. How could it be *if seeing is not involved in the process?* Yet how also can that 'disclosed' be safely other than the 'something already existing' that Thrift treats with such suspicion?

5   Conclusion

From the first, my argument has been that Thrift's notion of a 'hard-edge' to new managerialism within the contemporary university is problematic. Thrift's interest in focusing on the positive, and his rejection of those on the Left who simply criticise managerial practice, requires a division between good practice and bad, a binary every bit as problematic as that he questions – and I would say repeats – in his non-representational philosophy. The result is an inability to read the difficulty in institutional practices other than those few recognised as damaging: redundancies, cynicism amongst managers and the like. It follows that managerialism is not understood as a discourse of *transparency* intrinsically rooted in a disavowal of its own contribution to the truths it locates and manages. In my experience, for example, lecturers and administrators in the Higher Education sector in the United Kingdom are asked to 'drill down' ever deeper into the data that informs the institutional audit, gain an ever 'clearer' understanding of their successes and failures, this part of an ongoing process of self-reflection and reorganisation.[20] It does not matter, in this model, what the lecturers might have to say about this, or any other, practice. Just as in Thrift's account of the disclosure of harmony or its lack, the information disclosed within the audit is claimed to be as free from bias as it is subjectivity and language. There can be no argument with disclosure, thus understood. As such, it can be read as the fulfillment of the liberatory vision of 'The Lecherous Professor Revisited', the university of openness where all is brought out into the light. There is no need to address the way such knowledge is framed or think that, for a moment, there might be something that escapes even the brightest illumination. The free movement necessary to the limitless managerial university requires an absolute visibility, that is, a fully translatable and transparent 'object of free choice and rational assent in communication'

(Readings 1996, p. 184). I would argue that this is, in Thomas Docherty's terms, a discourse of 'fundamentalism', one that:

> has absolutely no difficulty in finding the relation between truth and reality, or between things as they are (ontology) and things as they appear (phenomenology). In short, fundamentalism claims a privileged access to the truth, and to an ability to translate evidence into truth...the logic of transparency is, itself, a form of fundamentalism, and it is one, crucially for my argument, that censors thinking, especially if these are claimed as matters of natural force or inheritance. (Docherty 2015, pp. 125–136)[21]

Where there can be no disagreement about meaning – where material truth is inescapable and divorced from signification, or, for that matter, where inheritance is taken to be an objective fact, independent of any subject position – dissent is cast out. And, indeed, alongside the story with which I began this book, I have heard, across the United Kingdom, an increased concern that university departments have come to understand dissent not as a virtue, but as a problem to be overcome: departmental meetings disseminating managerial decisions, rather than being spaces to work through policy; shrunken university councils obediently following the lead of Vice-Chancellors; Continuous Professional Development focused on how individuals academics are contributing to the university's priorities and vision, rather than encouraging original and diverse research; everywhere 'consultation' rather than dialogue. Here is Thomas Docherty again:

> [A]cademic and student bodies, as well as administrators – are expected to 'walk the line'. If they do not, they risk being placed in a position where the university authorities can jeopardize their careers by suggesting that their non-conformist statements threaten the brand, thereby menacing the standing and standardization of the university's reputation, and thus 'bringing the university into disrepute'. (Docherty 2015, p. 110)

As Bill Readings foretold twenty years ago, within this environment it is the discourse of 'excellence' that, above all, stands against dissent. 'Excellence', for Readings, is so successful within Higher Education, because it is applicable to anything, and thus can unify the university in a way that allows untroubled administration. It is a single unit of currency, capable of dissolving all difference. It is also obviously a good thing to pursue: again, who would be against excellence? It would be as unreasonable, as unthinkable, as questioning the outcome of 'disclosure'. Dissent is not then only limited through the overt stifling of oppositional voices within senate and departmental meetings, or by the removal of policies designed to protect free speech, but also the promotion of the kind of materialist self-evidence defended within *Non-Representational Theory*.

Counter to the arguments forwarded by Thrift, my call is for us not to turn away from a detailed reading of the production of knowledge. This, I would contend, means not joining with Thrift in turning from questions of subjectivity in favour of the seemingly more ecologically minded realm of the object. I find the following formulation by Judith Butler, a critic praised within *Non-Representational Theory*, helpful in this regard:

> To question... a term like 'the subject'... is to ask how it plays, what investments it bears, what aims it achieves, what alterations it undergoes. The changeable life of the term does not preclude the possibility for its use. If a term becomes questionable, does that mean it cannot be used any longer, and that we can only use terms that *we already know how to master*? (Butler 1997, p. 162)

For all its investment in futurity and its concern to avoid the pitfalls of humanist mastery, *Non-Representational Theory* can be understood to resist the open question of the subject. In this I am precisely not suggesting that a notion of subjectivity should be restored as the locus of truth: as Jan de Vos contends, this would merely be a repetition of the move to locate presence – the obviousness of 'excellence' – somewhere else (de Vos 2012, pp. 125–126). In my understanding, contemporary student surveys, and discourses of student voice and student-centered learning, are premised on a disavowal of the enabling contexts of signification, a demand for the student to express herself without compromise; the dream of 'transparent' communication (Readings 1996, p. 185).[22] Rather than establishing the student as rational consumer, I am suggesting that a concern with subjectivity can return the problem of knowledge to a discourse confident in its ability to move on from such concerns. It is through subjectivity that the gap or division that is constitutive of the knowing subject, and thus also the process of education, comes to light. My interest in subjectivity, in short, lies with its impossibility. Here is Ian Parker's recent overview of the issue:

> [subjectivity] appears in the development of psychoanalysis as an account of the self that questions the reduction of explanation to the conscious manipulative 'ego' as centre of reason and action; psychoanalysis rests on a

conception of the human subject as divided; divided between consciousness and the unconscious, and divided at the level of the unconscious, an unconscious which links each individual to others in contradictory lines of identification and hostility. You are not exactly who you think you are, and this opens the way to an emphasis on what is actually said, said to and with others, rather than looking to the master in the head who is able to decide what things mean. (Parker 2016)[23]

Throughout this present book, there has been an 'emphasis on what is actually said', rather than a move to escape from language, whether in the 'head' of the self-present subject or the realm of the object. Indeed, I read a tension between the projects favoured by Thrift and the psychoanalytic thus understood, even as the latter is figured by Peggy Phelan previously. Phelan claims that 'by locating the subject in what cannot be reproduced within the ideology of the visible, I am attempting to revalue a belief in subjectivity and identity which is not visibly represented.' As such, her concern is with the revaluing of a belief that is dependent on negation, the location of the subject in a *failure* of reproduction. The subject here cannot be taken in isolation from 'ideology' in so far as its location is only within the failure of this. For Thrift, despite his endorsement of Phelan, the interest is in practices that can be valued 'in and for themselves', those that are invisible and 'unmarked', yet knowable in a way that goes round the back of questions of phenomenology: reproduction is taken not to introduce an unavoidable, formative disruption, as all that is lost is treated with due respect only if it is left, and known to be left, 'just as it is' (Thrift 2008, pp. 110, 114). It is for this reason that, within *Non-Representational Theory*, any narration of the self is taken to be secondary and distorting. The truth of the subject is a matter of feeling and affect, inescapable, and wholly translatable. It is because the 'microbiopolitics' are under the threshold of the subject that they are available to all, and immune to critique: closure guarantees access, this ever the logic of the object within the university without limit.

Notes

1. See the introduction and Chapter 2 of this present book.
2. For more on this, see: Matthews, David. 2014. Thomas Docherty to face insubordination charge in tribunal. *Times Higher Education Supplement*, July 24; Colquhnoun, David. 2015. The University of Warwick brings itself into

disrepute -four times. Watch your tone of voice. http://www.dcscience.net/2015/04/08/the-university-of-warwick-brings-itself-into-disrepute-four-times-watch-your-tone-of-voice/. Accessed 1 November 2016; Grove, Jack. 2014. 'Simplistic' redundancy metrics criticised. *Times Higher Education Supplement*, October 16.

3. Although the relationship between Thrift's academic work and his role at Warwick has not been the subject of extensive discussion, a handful of blogs and academic papers have addressed the issue. Conor Woodman, for example, offers a double assessment, suggesting a simple disconnect between Thrift's philosophy and policy, while also registering that in '[r]eading some of his more jargonistic pseudo-academic writing, one is hardly struck by Thrift's firm opposition to injustice'. Woodman, Conor. 2016. Yobs, principles and Higher Education. http://warwickglobalist.com/2016/02/02/yobs-principles-and-higher-education-a-decade-of-nigel-thrift/. Accessed 1 November 2016. This latter is very much the conclusion reached by Camila Bassi's in her critique of Thrift's dismissal of Marxism. See Bassi, Camilla. 2010. 'The anti-imperialism of fools': a cautionary story on the revolutionary socialist vanguard of England's post-9/11 anti-war movement'. *ACME* 9/2: 113–137.

4. As I was preparing this book for publication, Thrift published a new essay on the university: Thrift, Nigel. 2016. The university of life. *New Literary History* 47: 399–417. In this work, a critique of 'totalizing models' leads to an interest in how the university can become 'united and increasingly different' (p. 414, quoting Félix Guattari). Along the way, Thrift expresses support for the discourse of 'impact' and for the influence of business on academic structures (p. 405), while satirising academic cynicism towards the present direction of travel, with its seemingly misguided notion that 'the paraphernalia of administration is a burden imposed by outside forces, especially when things aren't going the way academics would like and they are looking for things to blame' (p. 404). With its particular favouring of partnerships with private finance (p. 404), 'modest', piece-meal advances (p. 415), rejection of grand narratives, and promotion of enabling and benign universalizing structures (p. 414), it could be argued the primary influence on Thrift's work is as much Tony Blair as any of the poststructuralist thinkers to which it regularly appeals.

5. See The Boar. 2015. 241 members of staff earn less than the living wage. https://theboar.org/2015/02/241-members-staff-paid-less-living-wage/. Accessed 1 November 2016. Warwick has recently implemented a guarantee of Living Wage, however: McGrattan, Gillian. 2016. http://www2.warwick.ac.uk/insite/news/intnews2/2017_pay_award/. Accessed 1 November 2016.

6. For an extended list of texts arguing against the managerial university, see House, Richard. 2015. Research resource on the neo-liberal university.

http://www.criticalinstitute.org/wp-content/uploads/2015/02/Richard-House_Bibliog-resource-TCI.pdf. Accessed 18 January 2016.
7. Variously described as 'dazzling' and 'richly-textured', and widely cited in contemporary writing on theory, education, art and geography: Walshaw, Margaret. 2011. Non-representational theory as a vehicle for thinking about pedagogical experience. *Pedagogy, Culture & Society* 19/3: 485–490, 487; back cover endorsement to Thrift (2008).
8. See Gregg, Melissa and Seigworth, Gregory. 2010. *The affect theory reader*. Durham: Duke University Press; 2015; Roelvink, Gerda and Zolkos, Magdelena, eds. 2015. *Angelaki, Special issue: Sentient subjects: Post-humanist perspectives on affect*, 20/3.
9. See, for example, Massumi, Brian. 2002. *Parables of the virtual: Movement, affect, sensation*. Durham: Duke University Press; Massumi, Brian. 2015. *The politics of affect*. Malden: Polity Press.
10. Here it is worth noting a recent major addition to the field, published as this present work was going to press: Lesnik-Oberstein. 2016. The object of neuroscience and literary studies. *Textual Practice*. http://www.tandfonline.com/doi/full/10.1080/0950236X.2016.1237989. Accessed 1 November 2016. In questioning the material turn and the turn to affect across a wide range of literary approaches, including 'Literary Darwinism', Lesnik-Oberstein raises questions 'about how and why whole recent – and ongoing – debates about science and literary studies, about "interdisciplinarity" and its (im)possibilities and about "the history of theories of mind", manage to take place in strictly liberal-humanist terms; that is to say, for all the scrupulous open-mindedness often on display, deconstruction is, apparently, the – as it were – "theory of mind" whose name dare not be spoken. The central question for me here is not whether Literary Darwinism in and of itself is legitimate or not, but why deconstructive approaches in this particular debate are apparently relegated a priori to illegitimacy? Why and how are they not included in the debate? (Isn't that what a "debate" is supposed to be?); all the more as this has in many senses always been, in fact, their debate par excellence?' As the analysis proceeds, the rarely engaged difficulties and limitations of what Jan de Vos terms 'the ossification of the social' are rigorously worked through: 'In these views [of Elizabeth Barry, Lois Oppenheim, and Peter Fifield] interestingly and in some senses paradoxically, "humanity" is located not in subjectivity and self-doubt, but in an objectivity which is claimed to be "more complex" than "cultural or textual phenomena", while at the same time also being about language as somehow "personal" and not about a "system"'. Here I would also recommend a further important critique of affect discussed by Lesnik-Oberstein: Caselli, Daniela. 2010. Kindergarten theory: Childhood, affect, critical thought. *Feminist Theory* 11/3: 241–254.

11. Such inconsistency, I would argue, can be read throughout *Non-Representational Theory*. Thus Thrift is: committed to a 'constant war on frozen states' (p. 5), while privileging movement as that which 'captures... joy' (p. 5); promotes 'presence, closeness and tangibility' (p. 5) despite being 'most concerned with... banishing nearness as the measure of all things' (p. 17); and critiques theory that is 'enmeshed in textual metaphors' (p. 129), yet celebrates 'the production of new kinds of... formative spaces which act as a generalised form of writing on to and in to the world...' (p. 23).
12. Or, in the formula offered by Jan de Vos, this is a 'naïve materialism', unable to place textuality and fantasy at the site of the real (de Vos 2012, p. 85).
13. Thus, '[t]he formula *that is what you are* opens up the (albeit problematic) perspective of a subject looking puzzled at itself as an objectified thing' (de Vos 2012, p. 6). For Jan de Vos, this subject is an unaccountable remainder, a 'zero level subjectivity', or 'non-substantial space where once the subject was' (de Vos 2012, p. 90).
14. The shared fantasy in this case is between White March protesters, Hardt and Negri, and Academia.
15. The tension between a hard-impacted physicality and all that lies beyond can be further read through the aforementioned claim that there is a 'somatic currency of bodily stances'. The 'stances' circulate beyond themselves, are part of a wider structure, and it is this that is 'passed on'. For more on this, see the discussion of 'the trope' in the work of Carolyn Steedman in Cocks, Neil. 2014. *The peripheral child in nineteenth century literature and its criticism*. Basingstoke: Palgrave Macmillan, pp. 143–172. Steedman's idea is that the danger of a linguistic approach to history is overcome by situating difference within a given unit. This seemingly gets round the problem of a naïve faith in singularity and presence, while also protecting against a deferral that would disrupt the grounded materiality of the past. Difference is held within, yet, in my understanding, this is an arrangement subject to the very difference it would contain. Interestingly, a comparable move has been located in Readings (1996). According to Christopher Fynsk, Readings claims that the University is non-referential, yet ignores the reference situated within this non-referentiality: 'Here [Sam] Weber detects a problem. Doesn't the "self-reflection" implied in the movement and measure of excellence – albeit of an apparently extreme technocratic and bureaucratic kind – nevertheless constitute a certain kind of reference? Perhaps even the very kind of self-reference found in that which inaugurates Enlightenment thought, rather than in a "post-historical" present to which the Enlightenment tradition is irretrievably lost?' See: Wortham, Simon Morgan. 2006. *Counter-institutions: Jacques Derrida and the question of the university*. New York: Fordham University, p. 123.

16. There are further difficulties: without the ghostly status of the subject, 'stance' is a matter of repetition only, and in this fails to qualify as legacy, implicated, therefore, in the deathly iterations that define 'interpretation'. Here I would recommend again Sue Walsh's work on narratives of embodiment that assert 'essence (here the materiality of the body) as the grounds for action': 'yet since this "essence" is necessarily an effect of discourse, it can never ultimately be laid claim to "except in a language conceived of as secondary and as always already figural". This leads to a self-defeating and self-contradictory position, in which essentialism, while recognised as ultimately limiting and constraining, and so repeatedly critiqued, is also repeatedly reinstated as the grounds for action because the "sphere of political action [is] conceived of as literal, as functioning literally, as... detached from the rhetorical sphere of signifying practice". (Walsh 2015, p. 33)

17. A more thorough engagement with Readings (1996) is beyond the scope of this present book. It is worth noting here, however, that Readings could be understood to share with Thrift a distrust of 'representation', pp. 104, 187. It can be argued that there is a difference between the two theorists, however, in so far as Readings's non-representational theory does not claim to bring its object to the knowledge of the zero-level subject. Indeed, for Readings, as discussed earlier, it is the necessary gap introduced by 'the Other' that is the basic condition for education, pp. 189–193. A difference between my work and *The University in Ruins* can also be read, as the latter takes 'the Other' to be a demand that exceeds the instance. To question this, I would turn to Paul de Man, a critic praised by Readings, especially 'The Resistance to Theory', in *Yale French Studies* 63 (1982): 3–20. For de Man, the textual instance is at some stage necessary to what is nevertheless its necessary other. I am presently writing on this issue.

18. Here it might also be helpful to look at Thrift (2016). There is a central appeal to 'honour', 'duty' and 'obligation' (Thrift 2016, pp. 400, 413, 409). Again, I read this 'obligation' to be other than that suggested by Readings. For Thrift, the obligation is, for example, to transmit knowledge or to engage in local, charitable endeavour.

19. Elsewhere, Thrift quotes Wittgenstein stating 'how hard it is to see what is in front of my eyes', and further claims that 'to see what is in front of our eyes requires thinking – and thinking about thinking – in different ways' (Thrift 2008, p. 112).

20. This audit includes that related to emotional labour, I would contend. Much more could be written here about such labour, but for a reading that counters what I take to be Thrift's depoliticised assessment of the affective field, see Parker, Ian. 2015. The function and field of speech and language in neoliberal education. *Organization* 17/3: 1–7. I am very interested in exploring the question of the emotional in a further publication,

especially as it relates to the construction of illness within both neoliberal Higher Education discourse and work that positions itself against this.
21. See also Rolfe, Gary. 2013. *The university in dissent: Scholarship in the corporate University*. London: Routledge.
22. For more on this, see Lesnik-Oberstein, Karin. 2011. Introduction: Voice, agency and the child. In *Children and culture revisited*, ed. Karin Lesnik-Oberstein, 1–17. Basingstoke: Palgrave Macmillan. See also Natalie Fenton. 2011. Impoverished Pedagogy, Privatised Practice. In *The assault on the universities: A manifesto for resistance*, eds. Michael Bailey and Des Freedman, 103–110. London: Pluto Press.
23. Here Parker is concerned with 'the variety of ways [the self] is described rather than pinning it onto one particular bright theorist'. He discusses revolutionary events that are not predicted or controlled by individual leaders, and the notion of 'collective subjects', as also challenging and reframing, rather simply dismissing, notions of the self.

REFERENCES

Butler, Judith. 1988. Performative acts and gender constitution: An essay in phenomenology and feminist theory. *Theatre Journal* 40/4: 519–531.

Butler, Judith. 1997. *Excitable speech: A politics of the performative*. New York, London: Routledge.

De Vos, Jan. 2012. *Psychologisation in times of globalisation*. London: Routledge.

Docherty, Thomas. 2015. *Universities at war*. London: Sage Swifts.

Leys, Ruth. 2011. The turn of affect: A critique. *Critical Inquiry* 37: 434–472.

Lorenz, Chris. 2012. If you're so smart, why are you under surveillance? Universities, neoliberalism, and New Public Management. *Critical Inquiry* 38: 599–629.

Lynch, Kathleen. 2015. Control by numbers: New managerialism and ranking in Higher Education. *Critical Studies in Education* 56/2: 190–207.

Parker, Ian. 2016. Subjectivity: Saint Jeremy. https://fiimg.com/2016/07/11/subjectivity-saint-jeremy/. Accessed 1 November 2016.

Readings, Bill. 1996. *The university in ruins*. Cambridge, MA, and London: Harvard University Press.

Thrift, Nigel. 1997. The rise of soft capitalism. *Cultural Values* 1/1: 29–57.

Thrift, Nigel. 2008. *Non-representational theory: Space/politics/affect*. Abingdon: Routledge.

Walsh, Sue. 2015. The recuperated materiality of disability and animals studies. In *Rethinking disability theory and practice: Challenging essentialism*, ed. Karin Lesnik Oberstein, 20–36. Basingstoke: Palgrave Macmillan.

INDEX

A
Academics For Academic Freedom, 9, 40, 56
Affect, 13, 66, 68, 78, 81, 87, 89
Agora, 7, 17–37, 83
AI Media, 31, 37n18
Audit, 1–7, 12, 13, 13n3, 15n8, 15n13, 18–20, 34, 73, 91n20

B
Barber, Michael, 19, 35n5
Blair, Tony/Blairite, 18, 19, 88n4
Bologna Accords, 5, 20
Bullying, 8–9, 13, 15n16, 39–61
Burman, Erica, 42, 43, 59n6, 59n7
Butler, Judith, 71, 86

C
Collini, Stefan, 5, 13n2, 15n7, 35n4, 64
CPD, 3

D
Davies, Bronwyn, 19, 20, 27, 36n15
De Man, Paul, 13, 23, 91n17
Derrida, Jacques, 8, 28, 29, 32–34, 36n12, 37n22, 90n15
De Vos, Jan, 10–11, 42, 59n6, 72, 73, 86, 89n10, 90n12, 90n13
Digital learning/technology, 7, 31
Disclosive, 83
Docherty, Thomas, 11, 12, 15n16, 20, 21, 35n1, 85, 87n2

E
Ecclestone, Katherine, 8–10, 15n7, 39–61, 63, 64, 83
Email, 3–5, 14n5, 14n6
Eve, Martin Paul, 18, 34
Excellence, 2, 4, 5, 7, 8, 15n12, 20, 30, 34, 36n10, 85, 86, 89n10, 90n15

F
Father, 28–30, 74–78
Freud/Psychoanalysis, 71
Furedi, Frank, 40, 42, 52, 58n2, 61n15

H
Hayes, Denis, 8–10, 15n7, 39–61, 63, 64, 83
House, Richard, 5, 30, 42, 43, 59n6, 59n7

I
Inheritance/legacy, 28, 29, 44, 45, 75–78, 85
Internationalisation/Globalisation, 13n1

L
Left-wing, 8, 9, 21
Lesnik-Oberstein, Karin, 37n17, 42, 59n6, 89n10
Leys, Ruth, 68, 71, 74, 81
Lorenz, Chris, 11, 20, 36n16, 66, 67

M
Massumi, Brian, 68
Microbiopolitics, 68, 77, 78, 84

N
New managerialism, 4, 8, 10, 18–20, 35n7, 52, 59n4, 65–74
Noble, David, 19, 27, 28, 30
Non-representational theory, 9, 10, 12, 63–92

O
Object/Objecthood, 1–16, 17–37, 43, 50, 53, 64, 70, 72, 74, 77, 78, 83, 91n17
O'Neill, Brendan, 40, 54–57, 60n12
Openness, 3, 17–37
Ossification of the social, 72, 78, 82, 89n10

P
Parker, Ian, 11, 36n7, 37n21, 59n6, 86, 91n20, 92n23
Pharmakon/ scapegoat, 8, 29, 30, 33, 45, 73
Phelan, Peggy, 76, 87
Plato, 8, 28, 32, 34, 36n12
Polis, 8
Postmodernity, 58, 60n11, 64–74
Psychologisation, 10, 42, 57, 72
Purkiss, Diane, 7–8, 17–37, 40, 64, 83

R
Radical Humanism, 40, 52, 54–58, 64
Readings, Bill, 4–6, 8, 9, 13, 13n1, 15n12, 15n13, 20, 21, 30, 35n1, 82, 83, 85, 86, 90n15, 91n17, 91n18
REF, 2, 3, 13n1
Repetition/iteration, 10, 21, 23, 24, 32, 34, 43, 56, 65, 70, 74–76, 86, 91n16
Restorationist, 8, 40, 49, 53, 59n3, 83
Rolfe, Gary, 12

S
Sayer, Derek, 12, 13n1
Shotter, John, 79, 81
Space/place, 3, 7–9, 20, 21, 23–25, 27–29, 30–34, 36n12, 46, 49, 54, 69, 74–78, 82, 83, 90n13

Spiked!, 40, 48, 50, 54, 56, 58n1, 61n15
Spinosa, Charles, 80
Subjectivity/the subject, 10–11, 40, 41, 43, 45, 51, 52, 58, 59n6, 59n7, 69–70, 72, 73, 83–84, 88n3, 91n16

T
TED Talks, 31, 37n19
Therapy/therapeutic, 8–9, 39–61
Thrift, Nigel, 9–12, 51, 60n11, 63–92
Transparency, 1–16, 18, 19, 21, 31, 74, 83

U
University of Reading, 11, 14n4

V
Vision/visible/seeing/invisible, 3, 5, 7, 10, 21, 23, 28, 30, 31, 36n10, 78, 79, 81–84, 87

W
Walsh, Sue, 70, 89n7, 91n16
Wortham, Simon Morgan, 13n3, 37n22, 90n15
Writing, 23, 26, 28–30, 32, 35n2, 54, 72, 74–76, 88n3, 89n7, 90n11